# BEOWULF: THE MIDGARD EPIC

By JAMES MATTHEW BYERS

ISBN-10:1-945263-07-5
ISBN-13:978-1-945263-07-1

## PROLOGUE

In days of late, the olden Thanes
Were known abroad, those kings called Danes,
And warriors great, they lay in claim,
Great warriors, yea, in every name.
The Son of Sheaf, begotten Scyld
Took many captives in his yield.
With terror's grip, their stolen pride
10    He thrashed in all, all terrified;
Alone to Daneland, fresh and wild,
He traveled as a single child.
Hence coming from abandonment,
This Scyld took hold and up he went
Till riches poured from every side
With nothing sought for ere denied.
The people ruled from isle to isle
Beneath his sword would reconcile
To give Scyld ear and lend Scyld hand,
20    For his voice ruled in each command,
In pride and honor, valor's sting;
And all said, "Scyld, there was a king!"
This did not limit all he gave,
For God had heard, and God does save.
Thus in His giving to Scyld's gains,
He gave a new prince for the Danes.
Before this child, a lawless kin
Of misery this lot had been,
A kingless hoard, a sheathless knife
30    Until the Ruler of all life
Brought to the Danes a kingly prince
Whose honor spread in evidence.
By way and deed, Beow went on
Until his name the world was known.
Thus Scyld's son's name grew glory bound
Like none in Daneland ever found.
This Beow gave from Scyld, the king,
And did so young as golden rings
Brought fighters of his father's measure
40    Serving him, this Beow's treasure.
Wound and bound around his heart,
His father's soldiers did their part
And would arise in time of war
To answer Beow's warring score.
Hence wealth grew shaped by virtue's sword,
As all supplied Beow's accord.

Then God called Scyld, collecting him
Unto his death and life went dim.
Still strong and proud, unto God's hands
50   Departed Scyld from his Daneland.
His comrades bore him to the sea,
Unto the shore, his destiny
And in request, his last words hung
There spoken by Scyld's dying tongue.
His kingship worn in lengthy strides,
Scyld led the Danes through turning tides
Of yearly seasons long in float.
His soldiers bore him to the boat
Which waited in the harbor's grip,
60   Full icy timbers on the ship
Prepared for Scyld, this ring filled cast
Where many mourned as by the mast
The corpse of Scyld so gently lain
Received in full each earthly gain
Bestowed by those who loved their king,
This giving lord who gave each ring
And in the end received more back
Than any loot from planned attack
Could ever fill, had ever reaped,
70   As thus before his dead form heaped
His helmets, jeweled, crusted gems,
Alongside swords both broad and slim
With curves and hooks, a merit's girth
The likes Scyld knew not hence his birth;
Such coats of mail in silver light
With armor for his final flight,
Great treasures shining mast to helm
The likes not seen in any realm
Nor any time or place on earth,
80   Befitting their lord for his worth.
Through tears to hoist the banner high,
The golden banner breaking sky
And wind designed by those submitted,
His, a ship so finely fitted
None before, nay, ere again
Could claim such honor as a man;
No king sailed off before adorned
In such a way, more greatly mourned.
Begrudgingly, those fighters saw
90   Their lord adrift with no guffaw
Within their hearts, within their souls,

As on the waves, none had control
To say how far the tide would pull,
Yet they refused to leave the hull
Without a tribute steeped in gold,
Thus gave no less than ever told
Or heard of since, each giving full,
Those setting him off on the lull
Of waves and wind, much better than
100    When as a child he had no clan,
Arriving poor on Daneland's shore,
An orphan who had died much more.
Thus now a banner richly raised
By saddened hearts lamenting praised
The deeds of Scyld in their decree
As wave and waters of the sea
Took hold the icy timber's thrush
Within the somber soldiers' hush,
And pulled the vessel in their wake
110    While further out the banner's stake
Laid claim to where no ruler knew,
Nor hero as the deepest blue
Locked hold to lead their ruler hence
To places only God knew whence.

# 1

Then Beow ruled all Daneland's gate,
This son of Scyld, this lord o'er fate,
And ruled as well and long indeed
As Scyld had done, his father's seed
Implanted lovingly within,
120    This famous lord o'er Daneland's men.
Then he in suit brought forth a son,
A son to rule o'er everyone,
The mighty Healfdane, fierce and bold
Who led the Danes in legends told
With days of living long endured,
The kingdom settled and secured
Until his end when passing on
Four children and a king-filled throne,
Three princes guiding Daneland's hilt
130    In battle, war their blood-stained quilt,
This Hergar knowing ere he should
With Hrothgar and Halga the Good
In times of need fear not a thing,

These princes, three, givers of rings,
And lo, one daughter, Yrs her name,
Became the wife of Swedish fame
When given to Onela's hand
To be his queen and rule his land.

Then Hrothgar, next in line as king,
140    Led Daneland to bear glory's ring,
Such glory that in one accord
His comrades swore oaths by his sword
And kinsman did as well in length
While young men added to his strength
In swelling droves, and army's might
Triumphant o'er the darkest night.

Thus Hrothgar thought in great resolve
To build and forge what none could solve:
The greatest mead hall known to man
150    Beneath the reach of Heaven's span.
Within the hall, divided spoil
His hand would grant for each their toil,
From young to old, the old to young,
The finger's rings, the necklace hung
Round ruddy necks or golden coin,
Or mail on chest or girded loin
Divided, earned in every place
That Hrothgar sent them to deface
For Daneland's sake, the glory bar.
160    He paid them all for every scar,
But pasture's soil and common ground,
He left with life where ere was found
Thus sharing all that God had blessed
As soldiers in his gold were dressed.

So, ordered he the timbers lain
And tied and shaped from each domain
Where came his help, artisans schooled
In craftsmanship from lands he ruled,
This Hrothgar and the varied hosts
170    Who aided him from coast to coast
And, lo, before the hammer's fall
Beneath the rock and stone in wall
With crusted gem and shield and spear
The greatest mead hall did appear.
Most beautiful, designed delight
Of Hrothgar's wish sprung from his might,

Then all the world whom Hrothgar led
Subscribed to visions in his head
Where named he Herot, his crown,
180    A name spread forth to every town
And countryside in measure's worth
Until it spread o'er all the earth.

His prideful boast no man could match,
Thus Herot was quite a catch,
And soon a banquet large and grand
This Hrothgar gave in open hand
Filled full of rings, a treasure ball;
He gave and gave within his hall.
That towering and gabled place
190    Stood waiting, ere, for time's own pace
When war would burn, the leaping flame
Of brothers barred in feud and blame
When this, the loveliest of halls
Called Herot would duly fall.

A grueling monster, grim and harsh
Who lived inside the darkened marsh
Impatiently convened the night
Through painful howling bred in spite
As day by day the music rang,
200    Alongside harp strings' fretted pang
Amidst the muse's choral bang.
In loudest joy the poet sang
Of ancient dawn when all began,
Recalling how God made each man.
He shaped the earth by crafting plains
Where oceans spilled and hills remain,
Where trees and grass filled forest glens,
Where nations moved as God led men,
He set the light which blazed at noon,
210    He called the sun and carved the moon,
The corners of this earthly space
Were lush and full within God's grace.
And then, as now in joyous measure,
Soldiers sang of each their pleasure:
So, the men beneath the reign
Of Hrothgar lived devoid of strain
Or peril in his happy hall
Until the monster bade his call.

That demon being, fiendish brute,

220 Named Grendel, who would steal and loot,
Who haunted moors, and marshes wild
Beyond the fears of every child,
And made his home a Hell on earth.
From slimy swamps erupted birth
Set on by two, conceiving pair,
Those monsters born of Cain's affair,
Such creatures banished ere they trod
By way of He, almighty God
Forever punished in each breath,
230 Perused because of Abel's death.
Thus exiled, bitter, driven out
Were these that God had placed about
Away from men, shut off from light
They split into the darkest night,
A thousand evils, every one,
Destroyers lost before the sun:
Foul spirits, fiends, a goblin hoard,
And Monsters, giants, at the Lord
Opposed and angry, bent to kill
240 And thus disbanded from God's Will,
Yet God repaid their tainted blood,
Destroying them all with the flood.

## 2

And then, when darkness dropped its veil,
Came Grendel through the darkened dell
Inquiring what these soldiers do
When music stops, their drinking through.
Thus came the monster in his wrath
And entered in the doorframe's path
Unto the hall, the placement where
250 The soldiers slept, all unaware.
He found them nestled in their sleep
There, undisturbed, a peaceful deep
And unsuspecting sort of creed.
The monster's thoughts filled full of greed
In quickened manner, as his speed
Unleashed his claws to fill his need.
His frothing tongue hung loose and dirty,
Snatching men, in total, thirty,
Smashing, dashing hide and flesh,
260 These sleeping mortals in the mesh
Of Grendel's clutch, their bodies hanging,

Dripping blood, their entrails dangling
As he ran back to his lair,
Delighted with the night's affair.

At daybreak with its rising sun,
The soldiers saw what had been done,
And just how well this Grendel worked,
How from their sleep those men were jerked,
And wrenched from life; now nothing save
270   The bloodstained floor to be their grave.
Thus on that morning, gray and grim
This Herot had ceased to trim
The cups with mead, the plates with meat
As joy fast made its full retreat
And tears and sorrow in time spent
With mourning sang their sad lament.
And Hrothgar sat in mad despair,
He, sad this evil had come there
To Herot, a king in fear
280   Sat brooding o'er his loss in tears
Full knowing by the tracks in mud
And by the stains of brothers' blood
Some demon had performed this deed
Where he and his enjoyed their mead
With bitterness inside his heart,
He knew what tore his men apart.
His greatest fear for every friend
Came feeling this was not the end,
But more the start of death to men.
290   And that night, Grendel came again,
So set on slaying, in his veins
The hunger thirsted like a pain
Fulfilled by only killing people,
His lust born in truest evil.
Herot his patrons fled,
These fighters fast escaping dread,
And seeking each a different bed
For fear that they would wind up dead.
Thus knowing nightly when they slept
300   This Grendel came and cruelly crept.
So, safety equaled distance as
Their time in Herot would pass,
The only ones surviving ran,
Avoiding Grendel's wrath to man.
His hate had triumphed, Grendel reigned
As o'er the righteous he obtained

Dominion, many against one,
And this one, Grendel, he had won.

Alone, an empty, broken splinter
310   Herot stood twelve long winters
Muddled in the disbelief
Of Hrothgar's tears, his endless grief,
This king of Danes, with sorrow heaped
Upon his door by evil reaped
In dismal, grim repulsive bands
Described at best as sin-spawned hands.

Abroad the whale-road, misery
Became a song sung openly
Of Hrothgar's sorrowful lament:
320   How Grendel came and Grendel went
While relishing his bloody feud
Upon the Danes, his lustful food.
For nothing save their end in death
Would ease this Grendel, soothe his breath,
No price in rings or gold or land
Could stave his wicked, Hell-bent hands
Which paid the living in his deed
By tearing hearts and making bleed
These warriors Hrothgar ruled
330   In bitterness, his virtue fooled.
There no one asked for reparation,
Claws in motion, desperation
Bursting from the shadow's dark
And Hrothgar's heroes were the mark
This Grendel hunted, young or old,
The cowardly, the brave and bold,
His latent anger, cruel and harsh,
Where hidden, he lay in the marsh
Invisible, this beast unseen.
340   One killing creature, vile and mean,
Worked crime and torture against man
Alone, his conquest's grueling plan
Summed up bloodthirsty, greedy measure
Brought forth in a horror's pleasure.
Though that hall he called his home,
He dared not touch Hrothgar's throne,
Its glory bound by God above,
And Grendel could not know His love.

But Hrothgar's heart bled out in pain.

350 His best and noble felt his strain,
Then met in secret council where
In terror they combined their share
Of virtue and sought after clues
For what their fierce and bold could do.
Then some forgot God's good advice,
And brought their old God's sacrifice
In hope for Hell's supporting role,
In hope the Adversary's goal
Would be to drive their demon off,
360 That Satan would not laugh or scoff.
The heathen's dream, this all their hope
With Hell in heart, a knotted rope
Around their necks, a killing rod
For they knew not the truth of God,
Nor of His passing as He walks
Through all the earth, nor heard Him talk,
The Lord of Heaven and the earth.
They knew him not since ere their birth,
Nor heard His praises, glorified
370 Let them be weary, those denied
His peace, for trouble worn instead
Leaves them a life conformed to dread,
As in their hearts no solace found
Means they cannot be better bound!
All hail to those who willing, rise
To God and drop their dead disguise
And seek amidst their skin's release
The solace of our Father's peace!


# 3

So Healfdane's son in sorrow simmered,
380 Harsh and new, it seemed, it glimmered,
Wisdom's gift could not exact
Nor strength of arm destroy the tract
Which hung o'er king and all his people,
Cruel and violent, cold and evil.

In his home, Geatland's gulf,
Stood Hygelac's kin, Beowulf,
The strongest of the Geats' clan—
In fact, more strong than any man.
The earth beheld within its hold—
390 At last of Grendel's Lust was told

And quickly plotted ere he heard,
Proclaiming in with a noble word
To sail the sea, his might to bring
In aid of him, this famous king
The world called Hrothgar, helping him
And shedding light on spirits dim.
The wise ones did not dare regret
His going, nor did any fret,
Though by the Geats, greatly prized
400    He was, the omens finalized
In one accord, the outcome, good.
Thus Beowulf did all he could
To find the finest Geats seen,
And did so numbering fourteen,
Then led their way down to the ship
Prepared for voyaging their trip;
He knew the whale-road and its score,
Thus his crew would see Danish shores.
They set their sails, they hoisted mast
410    Beneath the Geats' logo cast
Upon the water's wave-bound biff,
Across the sea and under cliffs.
Those winding currents, ready bound
For action ere it could be found,
The ocean beating sand and reef,
The shining ship full of belief
In Beowulf, as in its lap
Rode fourteen Geats wearing caps
Or helmets with the fit for dreaming,
420    As with armor, shined and gleaming,
Headed safely in their boat,
Their hurried vessel swift afloat,
A bird on water, wings immersed
Beneath the waves, the path rehearsed,
As from the hull, the greeting seen
Exposed the hills, earth high and green,
Projecting upward, o'er the ground,
With much rejoicing in the sound
Of voices near that steep, rock face,
430    Their voyage ending by that place.
The Geats exited their ship
And pushed it in the sandy grip
Where it sat, tied, their armor shaking,
Chain mail shining, Geats making
Swift the ship moored in the sand
As they pushed on abroad Daneland.

The weather kept their ship from tossing,
God was thanked for such a crossing.

High upon a nearing wall,
440    A Danish sea-guard came to call
Within his watch upon patrol,
These armored men upon the shoal
And further inland, his eyes dining
On their shields and weapons shining;
He came down upon his horse
To seek these soldiers' current course.
He shook his hand which held his spear,
And asked, "Why have you landed here?
Who rules your hearts, each one of you,
450    Who sailed upon these waters blue
Within your ring-rung vessel's bough,
Which led you here before me now?
You, hear me! Here upon this gate,
These cliffs and shores, this oceans bate
That lures the tide in crashing bounds,
Long have I watched, have I been found
The guardian of all you see,
The one who keeps this Daneland free
From raiders, pirates, and from those
460    Whose rulers' wishes would impose
A mighty tariff in their grip,
Content to bank each yawning ship
In search of lives; in search of gold
Which Hrothgar keeps within his hold.
I dare say none have come before
So openly upon this shore.
And you, all soldiers by design,
Have given not a single sign,
Nor password offered by our Thane,
470    Nor word released from any Dane
To verify your landing here.
Lo, now I speak before my spear
And say of all the men on earth,
These eyes have not beheld a worth
Such as this man among you all;
None ever have held me in thrall.
No common person holds these weapons,
Lest my eyes behold deception.
Warrior, here speak your name,
480    And of your father, do the same;
No scouts advance, nor move ahead,

A further section than you tread
On Danish soil, from whence you came
Speak now, I say, here say its name.
And say it swiftly, swifter yet,
Or else the moment will regret
Your coming to this man-filled beach.
I say, speak now, in my spear's reach
Just who you are, from whence you hail,
490    And why you set your ship at sail."


## 4

Then Beowulf, the Geat's main,
Unleashed from in his deep domain
Heroic measures, spoken words,
And this is what the guardsman heard:
"My kith and kin, we are the same.
The Geats are our peoples' name,
And proud we hail our kingly lord;
We bow before Hygelac's sword.
My father bore a soldier's brand,
500    His name spread far o'er sea and land
Known for his mighty fighter's skin,
As well as leadership of men.
You've heard of Ecgtheow for sure.
O'er many winters would endure
His life; as all across the earth,
The wise still call upon his worth.
These words are meant to help convince
Your manner as we seek your prince,
The son of Healfdane, Daneland's lord,
510    Our friendship we extend, afford.
So help us, watchman, we beseech,
Initiate us with your speech!
Our mission, great, our business, grand,
No secret kept in my command
Meant for the king of Daneland's soil,
No darkness offered in our toil.
If truth be told, and told in truth,
The land is cursed, a vicious proof,
Some demon, vile in his repose,
520    Who steals the men when dreams bestow
Their mantel in the twilight's glean,
Then comes this hunter, swift, unseen.
It's spoken, guardsman, in his path

The Danes have met this creature's wrath;
Have been his harvest; worn his mark
And lived beneath the brooding dark
His terror brings amid his blight,
And does so each and every night.
Perhaps somewhere within my heart
530    When Hrothgar hunts throughout each part
A measure meant to bring about
A change and drive this devil out
Can find him there—if anything
May thwart what ails your famous king.
Yes, in my heart may Hrothgar learn
A means to cool his sorrow's burn.
Indeed, if not, then he may find
His suffering forever bind
Its knot around, a killing coil,
540    Awaiting on this Danish soil
For long as Herot still stands
Atop the hills, among your lands."

The guardsman turned, astride his horse,
These words becoming his next course:
"A warrior has in his reach
To be the judge of works and speech,
And keep this wisdom in his mind;
A surer place he cannot find.
I trust your words; I call you friend.
550    Keep on your armor as I send
You weapon bound beyond the sand
Into this realm, beloved Daneland.
Before you I, myself will lead
And guide you in the utmost speed,
Protecting you upon your trip—
My men will stay and guard your ship,
Their watchful gaze its safety now
Until its curved and chiseled prow
Departs in measures bold and grand
560    Across the sea to Geatland
Proclaiming in its brazen hold
The warrior, both fierce and bold,
Whose battle-might against the foe,
This creature plaguing us with woe,
Will shine within his victory.
He shall not die, he shall not flee,
Then leaves unhurt, the sea to roam
And takes our love within him home."

So further on these men explored.
570 Their boat lay anchored, tied and moored.
Atop each golden helmet hung
A wild boar's head whose gleaming sung
Its shining tune, a beaming shard,
Appearing as some rigid guard,
Like sentries poised amid their plight,
Preparing for their brutal fight.
They marched, with Beowulf beside
His men, all following the guide,
Until triangular designs
580 Of Herot seen in the shine
Reflected off its hammered gold—
That famous hall of legends told,
Majestic in its tower proof,
Made visible from glowing roofs
Now seen by those within the band
From far across its traveled land.

While turning there upon his horse,
The guide next pointed straight the course
Awaiting for Geat footfall,
590 To lead them to Lord Hrothgar's hall
For bold and brave in every kin
Who claimed such right among his men.
The guardsman spoke, words bursting through,
"My time has come to part from you.
Now may the Lord our God direct
Your journey, and o'er you protect
Your paths in coming and in going!
Now I must take leave, bestowing
By the sea my presence there,
600 To guard and watch its potent flare,
Ensuring that these coasts are free
Of trespass; that all raiders be
Repelled; all brigands bent off track:
Now to those coasts, I must go back."

# 5

The pathway shown lay paved in stone,
A cobbled anthem in the tone
Of Roman architecture's make.
The men arrived with much at stake,

Full-armored war skin, shining links
610     Of silver making clanks and clinks
Within their rhythm's iron tune
As on they marched. Sear-weary, soon
They set each broad, war-ridden shield
In rows along the wall's long yield,
Then stretched abroad the benches there
In light of Herot's full care.
Their war-garb rang amidst its shine;
Their ash-wood spears erect in line,
All tipped and ready from conception,
620     These, the Geat's glory-weapons.

Some proud soldier of the Danes
Asked who they were, their fathers' names:
"From whence have you brought forth your guild
Described in sight by golden shields,
By war-skins worn in silver flare
With helmets covering your hair,
And spears set out in lengthy rows?
I, Hrothgar's herald wants to know.
Before your feet set on this way,
630     No strangers coming since this day
Have ever been so brass, so bold.
And with your presence, I am told
Your pride and valor's speaking style
Say you are not castoffs, exiles.
No poverty brought you before
King Hrothgar, but your noble score
Within your heart's great golden gleam
For you are more than what you seem."

Responding was the well renowned
640     Combatant, he, the fighter bound
By honor in his noble sense
Before the Geats as their prince:
"We go where Hygelac may tread,
With him we drink and break our bread.
My name is Beowulf. My charge
Is meant for Healfdane's son in large,
Though for your country and your lord;
Should he receive our warm accord,
Saluting this great chief of Danes
650     And speak such words to ease his pain."

A prince of Danes known near and far

Replied, the wise and strong Wulfgar:
"Our famed and giving liege and king
Will learn of what you Geats bring;
This knowledge will pass to our king,
Our lord and giver of bright rings,
And then to you with all there heard
Shall I return with Hrothgar's word
And speak it here at your behest,
His answer born of your request."
In haste, he sped to Hrothgar's throne,
Where sat a king to many known
Now gray and old, amidst his fold,
And walking straight as customs told
Approached the king, who in his chair
Awaited Wulfgar's patient stare
As openly the silence broke,
And there his herald finally spoke:
"There are some Geats who have roamed
O'er highest waves, quite far from home,
And he who led them here with claim
Holds Beowulf to be his name.
They wait on what you have to say,
And bring this message here today
For you to hear, and you alone.
I ask you, here me from your throne!
The noble stature they so bear,
From weapons donned to armor's flare,
Holds to the finest craftsman's build—
Not one a beggar in their guild.
And Beowulf, their princely thane,
Who led them o'er the sea's domain,
Has me convinced, as with my eyes
I found him to be strong and wise."

# 6

The king of Daneland spoke this truth:
"I knew him when he was a youth.
His father, brave Ecgtheow, who
Because of his innate virtue,
The Geat ruler gave his one
And only daughter, making done
A pact with Ecgtheow back then—
This Hrethel making him his kin
And Hrethel fathered Hygelac.

660

670

680

690

Thus history has kept its track.
Now Ecgtheow's brave, noble son
Has come with something to be done
For me, an old and friendly king.
I've heard from those whose stories sing
Of treasures brought before the kin
700    Of Geats, then the games of men
In sport and humor found their catch
In racing or a wrestling match,
For those who made their ardent trip
Within the mighty battle grip
Of Beowulf, their going length.
He was amazing as his strength
Composed the likes of thirty men,
With matching courage found within.
Our Holy Father, as a sign
710    Of all His grace, of His design,
Has given o'er this Geat prince
To aid us and at last convince
The monster he will meet an end
Before the hands of our new friend.
My treasures, gifts and ample fuss
Will grant him praise from all of us.
In Haste, depart and bade them all
Be welcome at my beckon call.
And be sure Beowulf and they
720    See hospitality today!"

Then Wulfgar went beyond the door
With joyful messages secure
And spoke to those who waited there
The words King Hrothgar said to share:
"My king, the lord of every Dane,
Has bade me come and not abstain
In this, his message full of mirth,
To say he knows your noble birth,
And having come from far away
730    He calls you welcome here today.
Now go to him, and don't delay,
Keep helmets on, your full array,
But leave your shields and spears behind,
A symbol of the words you bind."

Then Beowulf rose with his kin
Providing orders to some men,
A simple duty to provide

A watch o'er weapons as inside
He led the others quickly past
740    The spaces Herot would cast
Until the throne of Hrothgar stood
And Beowulf approached its wood.
He stood abroad the great king's hearth,
His helmet shining without dearth,
The metal of his mail shirt gleaming
In the art of smithy's beaming
As the high art struck its chord,
While greeted he the Dane's great lord:

"All hail, Hrothgar! I am kin
750    With Hygelac, ruler of men;
My days of youth were glorified.
Now Grendel's name has horrified
The Geats in our Geatland
Who heard of his unearthly hand:
From sailors traipsing o'er the road
Of whales to bring the heavy load
Depicting Herot, the great
And glory bound hall, bent by fate
And circumstance now useless—worn,
760    For with the moon its halls are torn,
Deserted, life and light both gone.
My people said, the wisest known
Among them, that my duty rests
With Daneland's King and his dire test.
My strength they've seen with their own eyes,
From war's dark depths, they've seen me rise,
My enemies strewn in the mud,
As I stood, dripping in their blood.
I fettered five amazing giants
770    Into chains, the incompliant
Race itself, amid my girth,
I chased completely from the earth.
I swam the blackness of the night,
A hunter seeking monster's might
Beneath the ocean, one by one
I slew them all; the errand done
Or death would take me in its stead,
But I failed not as they are dead.
Together, Grendel and I from
780    The Geats are called, thus I've come.
Here, grant me king o'er this great land
Just one request! Afar, my band

Has traveled thus, and I came hence,
Oh soldiers' comfort, sturdy fence
For every Dane the eye can see,
This, grant and do not refuse me—
That I, alone with all my men,
May purge this hall of its chagrin.
The monster's scorn of men, I hear,
790    Is great, and thus it does not fear
Nor needs a weapon in its hand.
Nor will I when I make my stand.
My kingly liege Lord Hygelac
Might think me less if in the track
Of Grendel I strode bearing arms
To shield me from the creature's harm:
My hands alone shall fight for me,
A struggle for life's given plea
Against the monster that I face.
800    God will decide the time and place
And who is given death's cold grip,
Arrested on that final trip.
His plan will be the same, I think,
To enter here then gorge and drink
Of bloody bodies he has slain,
As he has done in this domain.
And if it is my time to die,
Then none should mourn and none should cry,
No corpse of mine will seek a grave
810    If these before us I can't save:
Our bloody bodies in the hands
Of Grendel will meet his demands
As to the moors he'll stop and hunch,
Then on our bones he'll nimbly crunch
And smear the scraps of skin from men
Along the walls of his foul den.
No Dane would fret or be less proud
If left to sew our resting shrouds,
Should Grendel's claw and teeth sink in
820    And give the beast the battle-win.
And should this death come take me, then
Return this mail to he, my kin
King Hygelac, return it all
That I, from Hrethel held in thrall
Designed by Wayland, send it back,
That all will reach King Hygelac.
This charge to you I give; I trust,
As fate unwinds the way it must."

# 7

830
Then he who ruled the Danes replied:
"In friendship, you won't be denied,
As Beowulf, based on reports
Of how your father found this court,
You come to us, and come in peace.
Now let me set your mind at ease.
So long ago, a bitter feud
Began out of the brooding mood
Your father found at Hathlaf's death,
The Wulfing warrior whose breath
Your father took: his countrymen,

840
Afraid of war, and for their kin
Should he return to his own home,
Then forced your father thus to roam.
Across the curving waves, he came
And found this place, the land of Danes.
I was a new king, ruling all
Within this golden kingdom's thrall.
My older brother, Hergar, was
A better man for Daneland's cause,
But died and dying surely beckoned

850
To me, being Healfdane's second,
First then through death's coronation,
Ruling firmly o'er this nation.
With my wealth, I brought an end
To what Ecgtheow could not mend,
The quarrel made a halting screech
When ancient treasures made their reach
Within the Wulfings' warring grasp;
Your father made this peace his clasp.
My tongue grows laden, and my heart,

860
With every word that I impart
Of all this Grendel has entailed,
The damaged wrought, this hall assailed.
You see yourself how small my ranks
Have thus become with Grendel's thanks,
And must surmise our loss incurred
Amidst the terror he has stirred.
For certain God Almighty could
Bring down his maddened lust for good!
How many times my men would boast,

870
With ale mugs jaunted high in toast

Providing courage once all drunk,
Full swearing when the sun had sunk
And darkness risen in the sky
By their swords thus the beast would die.
And then, when morning came in sight,
This mead hall glittered in the light
Quite drenched amid the torrid flood
Seen in the form of my men's blood,
The benches stained in deepest red,
880    That fiend's assault left each one dead
As all across the floor lay wet—
And even less, to my regret,
My soldiers stand decreased in ranks
With only death to give my thanks.
But to the table, Beowulf,
A feast awaits us to engulf
In honor of your bravery:
Come, let us toast your victories,
And speak of where your crew hails from,
890    As well our future yet to come."
Then Hrothgar's men provided for
The Geats spaces to secure
Their seating on the benches found
Within the mead hall's common ground
Where from the greatest to the least,
Together they would join the feast.
The keeper of the jolly task
Providing mead came holding flasks,
And poured its sweetness like a tune.
900    From time to time, the poet's rune
Sang clear and pure, his honey voice.
As one, both tribes drank and rejoiced.

# 8

Then Unferth loosed his tongue undone,
This soldier known as Ecglaf's son,
Who sat beside King Hrothgar's feet,
And spoke his words without retreat
(Vexation in the nomenclature
Served by Beowulf's adventure,
As with his unnerved approach,
910    And angered that without reproach
The whole of Daneland and beyond
Accepted this a truthful bond,

Expressed the anger Unferth felt
As from the fact beneath his belt
Was not the fame and glory known
By Beowulf to call his own.):
"So Beowulf, you are indeed—
The same fool boasting in his need
To challenge Brecca in a match
920    Of swimming for the victor's catch,
Both daring and quite young and proud,
Immersed beneath the ocean's shroud,
There risking lives for nothing but
The sake of danger's torrid rut?
The Elders spoke against your stride,
But none could check such foolish pride.
With Brecca swimming at your side
Along the whale-road's seamless glide,
Your eager hands pulled even pace
930    Across the ocean's open face.
Then winter spun across the span
Of water, as your bodies ran
Where waves so willed to push and thrive,
As there you struggled to survive
For seven nights that seemed so long
Amid the ocean's wicked throng.
And at the end, it was not you
Who wore the victor's burning hue.
The sea had brought him close to home,
940    Within its brewing, bubbling foam,
To southern Norway, near the land
Of Brondings, where his ample hand
Claimed rule and all gave him their love,
His treasure piled high up above
As from the threat of darkened evil,
He protected towns and people.
Promising to out-swim you:
The son of Bronstan's boast rang true.
Your battles won are luck, I say,
950    But Beowulf, just one night's stay
Within this hall will change your luck,
If Grendel's presence comes to shuck,
Should here the fierce unholy beast
Find you and choose you as its feast."

When Unferth's tongue at last was done,
His answer from Ecgtheow's son
Came fast and firm, Beowulf's speech

Delivered to each Dane in reach:
"Ah! Unferth, friend, your face is hot
960    With ale, and seems your tongue has not
The means to speak the simple truth
Nor offer any simple of proof
Of Brecca's doings. But I say
The truth is simple. Here, today
I tell you not a single man
Who braves the sea swims as I can,
Nor has a strength the likes of mine.
When we were two youths in the brine
We boasted—we were both unwise
970    To all the perils in disguise—
That we would risk the depths at sea,
And so we did this openly.
We both agreed in one accord
To simply bring a naked sword,
Prepared for whales or razor teeth
And beaks of needlefish beneath.
He never left me once behind,
Swam faster o'er the wave's incline
Than I could, and I chose to stay
980    Beside him as we made our way.
Near him, I stayed for five long nights,
Until a flood served us its plight
And separated both of us;
The frozen sea surged in a fuss
Around me, darkened, then the wind
Picked bitterness, the northern bend
From which it hailed, with savage waves.
Then Creatures stirred from murky graves
Where they had been within the keep
990    Of days unnumbered in their sleep—
And hammered links of iron bent
Into the shape of metal spent
Within the forms of chain mail worn,
The shining metal's gleaming shorn
Across my breast, this kept my breath
And saved me from untimely death.
A monster seized me, drug me down
In haste, intent to surely drown
Me, swimming with its gangly nails
1000   Which in my flesh were thus impaled.
But fate led me to find its heart
As with my sword I hacked apart
Its hold and found myself born free;

I fought that beast there in the sea
Until at last the waters spied
Its floating flesh, for it had died.


## 9

Then other beasties crowded round,
Attacking me in fits unbound.
I served them as was right to do,
1010 Thus offering the metal hue
Aglow amidst my razor's edge.
But in my offer's noble pledge
I think the feast did less than please
These monsters bred of foul disease,
Their evil bellies never full
With banquet-rich food, flesh, nor skull,
There thrashing at the gifts from me
While at the bottom of the sea.
By morning they slept on the shore,
1020 Atop their backs astride their gore,
As by the gifts from my swift hand
Their blood lay strewn upon the sand.
Thereafter, sailors traveled o'er
The whale-road fearing nothing more;
No, nothing stopped their passing o'er
The open waters anymore.
Then God's bright beacon in the east
Appeared as next the waters ceased
Their motion bound by waves in tow,
1030 Made still and calm beneath; below,
With land before my open view,
The wind-swept cliff—walls jutting through
Before the edge along the coast.
With much good reason do I boast
As fate will save the living when
By their own hand they fend death's grin
Alone, not with another's aid,
As I have done; my works displayed!
So luck or not, the number nine
1040 Gave total to those beasts in line
Upon the shore which by my hand
Met death and wound up on the sand.
What man can boast from underneath
The arch of Heaven, fending teeth
In darkness where his life is sought,

Enduring misery while caught
In places harder pressed to leave
Then surface, and he does not grieve?
Yet I survived the open sea,
1050   Smashed monsters' jaws who came for me,
Then arched my arms in full degree
To swim home ending my journey.
The waters swiftly flowing kept
Me going as they duly swept
Me on and on within their toil
Until I hit on Finnish soil.
No legends, myths or simple tales
Of you have stormed the road of whales,
Unferth, which tell of clashing might
1060   With terror; contests in the night!
The battles Brecca waged in war
Were never close in any score;
You could not match me, nor could he-
No boast is meant, but you can see
That what is said here now to you
Is nothing less than what is true.
And more, I say: those who you slew
Were your own kin, your brothers who
Were murdered. Words and brains won't aid
1070   Your soul; your suffering displayed
In flaming hell, Unferth, so know
Your torment's end will never show.
Proud Ecglaf's son, if your two hands
Were quite as hard, your heart's command
As fierce as you would like to think,
No fool would dare to even blink
An eye in sense to raid your hall,
Pierce Herot and he whose call
You run for, he the ruling one,
1080   The way this beast Grendel has done.
But he has soaked in terror's flare,
Discovered that without a care
His lust can melt with every bite
Of flesh he steals from you each night;
No opposition he's found here,
Just food to stave his hungry leer.
He murders as his want to do,
No mercy given when he's through,
Devouring his fleshy feast,
1090   Expecting none can tame his beast,
His inner yearning to fulfill,

Without a quarrel, those he kills
From any here amongst the Danes.
We Geats soon will show him pain
And courage bending idle prattle
Into strength tested in battle.
When the sun again breaks light,
And dawns another day from night
Eloping o'er the southern rise,
1100    Then any Dane can rub their eyes
And know behests from Hrothgar's call
Means safely they'll endure this hall:
For what I say soon shall be known—
That evil from this place is gone!"

The gray-haired Hrothgar, brave and bold,
Found merriment in what was told
By Beowulf before them all
Within the confines of his hall,
And surety set safely in,
1110    Believing Beowulf could win,
That Grendel could indeed be killed,
For Beowulf was strong and skilled.

The sound of laughter rang aloud
As mugs of mead met, smug and proud,
In gleeful manners, next to balk
As men brought forth their fervent talk.
Then Wealhtheow, King Hrothgar's queen
In gold-ringed garb stood in-between
To welcome these men from afar;
1120    A noble woman's noted par,
She lifted high a mug in toast
First praising Hrothgar as their host,
Then from her grasp she let it slip
And pressed it to her husband's lips,
Full wishing him joy in the feast.
The lord of all the Danes released
His blessings as he deeply drank.
Then as a measure meant to thank
The soldiers for their mirth and heart,
1130    The queen then gave a courtly start
By pouring beer, an ample sup,
From out the jeweled crested cup,
Until the bracelet-wearing queen
Had poured the mead to every seen
Before her, leaving just one more,

Then finally she stopped to pour
The mead for Beowulf to taste.
Her manner spoke in joyous chaste,
Saluting Beowulf, the great
1140    And mighty Geat prince, whose state
Exuded battles to be won,
Then she thanked God for all He'd done,
For placing in her hands the deed
Of giving o'er the precious mead
To one who would defeat the evil,
He, the hero for her people.

What she poured, he drank in mirth,
The son of Ecgtheow by birth,
Assuring Daneland's queen with truth:
1150    His heart was firm; his hands were proof:
"When o'er the whale-road we set sail,
My brothers and I, I knew well
That for me here my purpose was
To fight and win for Daneland's cause
Or die in battle in the grip
Of Grendel sensing my life slip.
In courage let me live each breath,
Or in this hall embrace my death!"

The woman found herself engrossed
1160    By every word, his gracious boasts;
Thus Wealhtheow moved swift in stride
And nobly found her husband's side.

The feast continued, loud and bold,
As in the days of legends told
With laughter spewing underneath
The cords of music cloaking grief
Along with kinsmen swapping tales
With every swish and swig of ale.
1170    Then Hrothgar, son of Healfdane, rose
With sleep-filled eyes intent to close;
For now, the sun had come and gone,
And Grendel's presence would be known
In Herot, his presence felt
When in the darkness, evil dwelt
And ruled, freed up, there given birth,
Loosed from the net which veiled the earth
To slither in the black, unfurled,
While wreaking havoc on the world.

1180    Then Hrothgar's war-kind rose with him.
        He went before the Geat, grim
        In undertone, yet full of hope
        That Herot would soon elope
        Disaster as he gave his hand
        To Beowulf, and wished command
        Of every inch within his hall
        Would be the Geat's to enthrall.
        And with no further preparation,
        There he gave this declaration:
1190    "Not since I could grasp a shield
        Has any been allowed to wield
        Control of all within my reach,
        None granted what I here beseech
        Upon your shoulder's weighty care.
        Make this, the best of mead halls flare
        In freedom as you claim its name
        As yours, and bring it not to shame,
        Delivering from evil plight
        These halls, and turn the wrong to right
1200    By breaking day upon this night.
        With glory in your heart, now fight!
        Purge Herot and when you sail
        To Geatland amidst the gale
        Of gusty wind, taut in its pull,
        Your treasure-holds will all be full."

## 10

        Then Hrothgar, Daneland's guiding chief,
        Made way from them to seek relief
        As all the men within his keep
        Did likewise, seeking peaceful sleep;
1210    His queen had gone before he tread
        The pathway to her side in bed.

        It came to pass, as men would learn,
        That God gave Beowulf his turn
        To guard the hall, this Herot,
        From Grendel's doomed, impending rot
        And be a sentinel before
        The Danes; to make them all secure,
        And be a shield to stand the test,

A place where Hrothgar could find rest.
1220    And Beowulf stood firmly placed
In highest favor by God's grace
Which added to the growing length
Amidst his courage and great strength.
He stripped from off his torso's keep
The shining mail with one full sweep,
Abandoning its long-time place
As next to it to fill the space
He placed his helmet and his sword,
Which had been hammered in accord
1230    As want and were those weary days,
Its hardest metal full of praise,
Then gave the rest, armor and all,
To one to guard until his call
Broke through the morning's beacon ray.
And then, beside where he would lay
He opened up without refrain,
And to them all he thus exclaimed:
"This Grendel is no braver than
Myself, nor stronger than I am!
1240    What need have I to use my sword,
For that would sooner halt his hoard
Of malice to an end in ease.
No, I shall not, for it would please
My honor to use just my hands;
God's gifts to give him reprimand.
The beast is bold and known abroad
As one who fights against the odds,
But claws and teeth would not avail
Against my shield, fists not prevail
1250    When pounding down upon my blade;
A hapless brute he would be made.
No, I shall meet him empty handed,
Less across his heart is branded
Such a fear its beating fails
When I am seen upon his trail,
A fighter waiting weaponless,
No fear within me to possess.
Let God within His wisdom's might
Extend His hand to whom He might,
1260    Rewarding one, as one shall lose,
His blessings on whom He will choose!"

Then Beowulf, the battle-brave
And whale-road weary aptly gave

Grendel

His head unto his pillow's care,
As did his soldiers waiting there,
As ready as they each could be,
These men who crossed the open sea,
Beside their lord unsure within
If they would see their home again.
1270     Its high walled towns and friends of old
Since days when youthful stories told
Enthralled them, mesmerized and dazed,
This home where each of them were raised.
Each thought of how this Grendel crept
And murdered all the Danes who slept
Where now the Geats made their beds
And wrestled these thoughts in their heads.
But God's great wrath was stacked upon
The monster, thus good fortune shone
1280     Upon the Geats ere they lay;
One man would hold the beast at bay
For Grendel's debt of weighty sin
Would soon be paid and they would win.
Who doubts that God in all His might
And wisdom calls the day from night
And holds the earth within His hands,
Discerning o'er all He commands?

Enshrouded in the cloak of night
The monster took to fiendish flight.
1290     Within the hall all fast asleep,
The fighters hoped that God would keep
Them safe from evil, guarding them
From death until the Father's whim
So, called them unto death's embrace.
But there within that darkened place
Lay Beowulf, awake, alert
And eager for the coming hurt
Which would be Grendel's, head to feet,
And knowing soon that he would meet
1300     His enemy, his anger grew
With every thought, anon, anew.

## 11

Out from the marsh and rotted logs,
The misty hills and sinking bogs,
Arose the one God's hatred clothed,
Rose Grendel, bloodlust fully posed

In hopes to catch and clip and kill
As many as would suit his thrill
In Herot, that hall on high,
Delighted, knowing men would die.

1310    He quickly moved amid the plight
Of cloudy cover through the night,
Up from his swampy, gloomy hold
In silence to the shining gold
Of Herot to make his call
Upon the men within the hall.

So many times he'd been to slay,
Quite well he knew the well-worn way—
But never, once before nor after,
Found within such planned disaster
1320    Waiting in the guarded post,
A harsher greeting from his host.

In joyless angst, he came for more
As eagerly he sought the door
The way he had those times before,
Thus snapped it open to procure
His heart's intent, as angrily
He crossed the threshold readily.
With speed, he strode across the ground,
His snarling features tight and bound;
1330    His eyes bulged out, a fearsome sight,
Embedded with an eerie light.
He stopped, then seeing war-men sleep,
All nestled snuggly in their keep.
And in his heart, fiendish delight
Set in, and he indulged the sight,
Intending to tear life and limb
From those left unaware of him
By morning's light; the demon's brain
Grew scorched with thoughts beyond the pain
1340    His claws would wreak, desiring food
To fill his belly's lustful mood.
But fate decided differently,
And Grendel was not yet to see
The present mold the die had cast,
And thus this meal would be his last.

The evil steps the being took
Were seen by human eyes that looked,

Awaiting in all that they saw—
To scope this creature's horrid claws.
1350 Then Grendel lashed his claw to snatch
The nearest Geat he could catch,
And tore the flesh from off his bone,
His body sliced by razors shone
Within the dimness as the teeth
The creature bore, without relief,
Then drank the blood from in the veins
And ate till nothing yet remained;
Till death found teeth bound in a rut,
As jaws closed up and snapped life shut.

1360 Then reckless, he let greed endure
And moved to make his mark secure
By feasting on another man,
But this was not to be the plan
For who he bade his gut enjoy
Was not akin to sleep's employ.

This Beowulf, in wakeful stance,
Became the monster's circumstance—
Who found himself indeed the one
Within the grip and out of fun,
1370 His claws pushed back behind and caught
In Beowulf's imprisoned taught
And mighty hold, who leaned upon
The arm of Grendel, pressing bone.
That evil minion, criminal,
Knew all at once his plate was full
For not a place on earth remained
Such hands as these to bring such pain;
His head grew full with fearful fright—
But nothing there amid the tight
1380 And painful clench his tendons nor
His claws, nor self could dare endure
To wrestle free from in the clasp
Placed under by this human's grasp.

Emancipation from the clutch
Of Beowulf engorged in such
A manner as his only thought;
His marsh's freedom all he sought
To bear away and run and hide.
His quest in Herot denied
1390 For never had this finest hall

Held such a man within its walls.

But Beowulf remembered well
His final boast, his wordy sell
And stood upright to halt the fiend
From fleeing; kept him quarantined
Within his grip till Grendel's claws
Began to crunch and snap in awe
Of heavy wonder in those hands
Which closer forced the beast to stand
1400    And bend unto the hero's might.
The wicked beast attempted flight,
Without the wish for human skin,
Just freedom he desired then;
His talons crushed, his movement stalled.
That fateful trip within those walls
Became a scourge of misery
To Grendel as he could not flee!

The creaking roof began to sway
As Herot boomed underway,
1410    And every Dane within it shook
In horror as the battle took
A dip, a turn down every aisle
There, Sensing none could reconcile,
Livid, crazed, and rather nimble.
Herot's walls barked and trembled,
Wonderfully designed to stand
Against the forces yet at hand;
Its shaped and fastened Iron walls,
Inside and out in beauty's call,
1420    Continued to hold firmly still,
Its benches toppled, then they fell
Upon the floor, each golden board
Beneath the fury-frenzied horde
Of Beowulf and Grendel's fight.
Those architects had crafted might
Within the walls of Herot
To hold to any battle brought
By armies seeking to corrupt
Its beauty; only flame's abrupt
1430    Induction to its wooden base
Would ever move it from its place.

The rising noise brought sudden change
And roused the Danes within its strange

And feral howl, creating new
And fitful terror from its brew,
Which bade them shake and quake within
Their beds as screams ripped out again
Of God's vile enemy who sang,
Somewhere in darkness, cries of pain
1440 And knowledge born of dire defeat.
The moans no longer made retreat
From Grendel's throat, hell's hostage bound
Amid the arms of him now found
To be the strongest man on earth,
This one held Grendel by his girth.

## 12

That powerful and mighty lord,
In everything he could afford,
Gave all he had to stay the beast
Until its life force was released,
1450 Aware that something of this brand
Would only curse all of Daneland.
Then Beowulf's crew cut the thread
Of sleep and roused from out their beds,
Their ancient blades held high and stout,
Determined to help their prince out.
Bravado raged within each man
But none could levy out his plan;
Though they could slash at Grendel's side,
Could plunge each blade and swing out wide,
1460 The path within him was denied.
No matter how each soldier tried,
The keenest steel could not begin
To barely even scratch the skin
Of Grendel, for through sin's deception
He bewitched all mankind's weapons,
Spells that dulled the sharpest blade.
And still his time would soon be made
Complete, his days on earth drew nigh,
Full knowing soon he was to die;
1470 Embarking on one last advent
To hell below without consent
Or penance to the waiting jaws
Of much, much worse than Grendel's claws.
Now revelations settled in—
This one who once afflicted men—

What trouble brought his feud with God:
His strength that once had been his rod
Broke free of him and evanesced,
His claws no longer he possessed,
1480   Bound fast by Hygelac's delight
Who tore them with his unbound might.

The demon's hatred rose, there shown,
But now his strength had all but gone.
He writhed in horrifying pain
As bleeding sinews, bursting veins,
And places deep within his shoulder
Snapped and toppled like a boulder
Falling from a crevice, high,
As muscle split and ripped awry
1490   From bone until at last it broke.
For Beowulf, the battle spoke
In unheard words of victory:
Though Grendel managed yet to flee,
But wounded in such manner, fled
Unto his marsh consumed with dread,
And knew his days were all gone by,
Aware once there he'd fall and die.

And after feudal, bloody sport,
The Danes exhaled at this report
In laughter full of mirth and glee.
This Geat from across the sea,
Brash-winded, strong and brave beyond
All men had managed to abscond
The wickedness; the foulest rot,
And purged the dens of Herot.
Quite thrilled with all his long night's duty,
There within that great hall's beauty,
Beowulf had served his boast;
His promise to the Danish coast;
The Geats' prince had stilled the beast
Who haunted once the great hall's feasts,
Had ended grief and sorrow's pang
Brought on the Danes by Grendel's fangs,
Now Hrothgar's suffering would end
As through this triumph, joy would win,
And not a single Dane refused
To doubt the victory, amused
And staring up below the roof
Where hung their only needed proof,

The devil's claw, his shoulder and
His arm at Beowulf's command.

## 13

And then, when sunlight broke the shroud
Of darkness, came a massive crowd
Surrounding Herot, the hall
Of halls, these soldiers come to call
From far off kingdoms, rulers and
Their kings and princes, come to stand
Before the monster's swerving tracks.
They passed their gaze not looking back
On sorrow for the creature's health,
Felt no regret for Grendel's wealth
Of pain endured, and went to trace
His bloody footprints in that place
Which led them to a murky ledge
That emptied in the water's edge
Where he had lugged his dying shape,
Aware from death he'd no escape.
The bloody water teethed and toiled;
Those crashing waves that steamed and boiled
From off the heat of sorcery
Which burst from in his vein's debris;
But swirling tide had hidden death
Beneath the murky, dismal breath
Pushed up, around, and out like fog
Erupting in that filthy bog,
Somewhere below where once he dwelled,
The beast had crossed the mouth of hell.

The old and young rejoiced alike,
Rejoined their mounts or chose to hike,
1500    Then turned aside their journey's track,
And slowly made their journey back
To Herot, prepared to tell
How Beowulf brought down to hell
The beast, and told this o'er and o'er.
No other man on earth, they swore,
Nor underneath the open sky,
Nor seas where many went to die,
Not north or south, nor east or west,
Could any find a man to best

1510 This warrior designed to reign
   O'er men, to rule o'er earth's domain.
   But none meant Hrothgar any less
   By praising Beowulf's prowess!
   And entertainment found its place
   As these men let their horses race.
   When paths divulged in single rows,
   Such brilliant steeds would heave and ho
   In frantic pace on down the road.
   And some aged soldier here or there
   Whose gift of wordy syntax flare
   Brought forth the tales of ancient men;
   Of heroes long remembered when
   The stories passed from man to man,
   Unleashed the past, as stories can.
   Thus here the old combatant's story
   Wove a net in worded glory
   Honoring the noble deed
   Of Beowulf from those he freed,
   The lyrics dripped like liquid mead,
   As sweet as honey, swift in speed,
   And fit the poet's worded quill,
   Expressing his dogmatic skill,
   Aloud his new song shaped its ring,
   Created ere the man would sing.

   And all the old songs he knew well,
   And sung them likewise; cast his spell—
   Adventures wrought by Siegmund's hand,
   The well-known battles in the brand
   As only he, the son of Vels,
   With splendid glory would excel.
   And conflicts, too, against the plight
   Of evil's treacherous delight
1520 That not a living soul had known,
   Except one, Fitla, who had grown
   In combat's weary battle stride
   While fighting at his uncle's side,
   A noble nephew tested true;
   A plucky youthful fighter who
   Gave full attention ere he heard
   His Uncle Siegmund speak the words
   Recounting mighty battles won,
   And deeds of valor he had done,
1530 In all the days the two would spend,
   Reciting to his dearest friend.

Such tales were told of giants slain,
Never to roam the earth again,
Removed by way of Siegmund's might—
Thus long remembered were his fights,
His fame beyond both life and death,
His noble stand in dragon's breath,
A dragon rich in gems and stones.
Thus Siegmund faced the beast alone
1540    When lo, he pushed the gray stone back
And entered on the dragon's track,
The dreary hole where its head hung,
Then raised his sword up high and swung
His blade the likes of ten men's strength
And sliced the great wyrm's neck in length
From top to bottom, forcing through
Until the sword tip came in view
Astride the mat of blood and gore,
Completing thus a mighty chore,
1550    Then pushed the blade back once again
And flung it with an extra spin
Encapsulating victory,
As with the thrust of his melee
The dragon's head flew sheer across
Its cavern in this final toss
And wound up pinned by Siegmund's blade,
A trophy for all times displayed
Upon the wall within its den.
With courage passing other men
1560    In line with strength unparallel,
Soon Siegmund found that he would dwell
Amid the treasure hoard he earned,
Great piles of gold where ere he turned,
And gems the likes the world not seen,
With rings galore for him to glean.
He loaded all aboard his ship,
Departing for the lengthy trip,
His beaming cargo filled the hold
With every type of gem and gold.
1570    Back in the cavern lay the beast
Whose blood, like acid, was released
Which singed the scaly dragon's hide
Until its shape no longer spied
By all the eyes of rats and bats,
For it had evanesced such that
Its very bones no longer shone,
No teeth, nor tongue, nay, it was gone.

No hero nor no kingship there
Knew greater fame than Siegmund's flare;
1580  His name grew known by virtue's fate,
And by his wealth, his fame was great.
There kept before him quite a king
Whose might and honor once packed sting,
But fallen under pride's abode
This great king failed, this Heremod.
His ego burned and victory
Came from his hated enemy
As exile forced him to the Jutes,
Where on their swords his life, thus moot,
1590  Fell underneath the throws of death.
That life had hated every breath,
For sorrows spread in misery,
And living with his enemy
Bore no avail for sorrows spread,
And troubles heaped upon each head
He ruled, for he seemed to despise
The words fair warned by those deemed wise,
Thus founded all his kingdom's might
On ego which fell prey to plight.
1600  A ruler birthed unto a crown,
Well-known abroad in every town,
His treasure hoard a beaming pile,
And warriors stretched mile to mile,
Yet these things made his manner swell
Until his actions spoke of hell
For pride will go before its fall,
And thus Heremod ignored the call
Of any voices but his own.
His death, deserved, gave up his throne.
But Beowulf, this well-loved thane,
Came only in friendship's domain,
No worry, fret, nor fear within;
But Heremod had followed sin,
And did so, never righting wrong,
As told within the poet's song.

The horses raced in any chance
1610  Begotten by their circumstance
Along the gravel-laden road,
Delighting those free from the load
Of Grendel's weight. A new light shone
And then the morning soon was gone.
The band of soldiers, sharp and brave,

Came on rejoicing Grendel's grave,
And found the walls of Herot,
Intent to sing the hero's plot:
Of Beowulf and wonders worn
1620    Atop his head, triumphant, shorn
And men could stop and stoop and stare
At Grendel's arm piece hanging there.
Then Hrothgar rose from off his throne
Beside his wife, for it came known
That Beowulf and all his men
Were there to call on him again,
And many joined the king's parade.
Then sweet Wealhtheow's presence made
The scene complete, his wife and queen,
1630    With all her maids stood in-between
The king and those now eagerly
Awaiting news of victory,
Then everyone begot footfall
As they walked to that splendid hall.


## 14

Atop the stairway, Hrothgar stood
And stared at what they all deemed good:
The claw of Grendel hanging where
The gold-trimmed roof met with the air.
He cried aloud: "Let God be praised!
1640    Too long we sunk in hate's malaise
By way of Grendel's daunting mire;
But God Almighty will expire
The doubt by miracles His Hand
Has wrought at naught but His command,
His wonders make the weak to stand,
For Midgard Rests within His hands.
All hope seemed lost within my care,
No words to fuse continued prayer,
No, nothing thus expected I
1650    But this misfortune and to die.
An empty, bloody Herot
Loomed nigh from all death had begot;
The wise men guiding me by word
Found naught but dread, despair I heard
From every lip which could not purge
My heart nor hall from Grendel's scourge.
No hope to cling or hold on to,

For nothing came from wisdom's view
As every wise man in accord
1660 Felt we could not beat with sword
Or strength within the demon hive,
Nor unclean spirits, or survive
The onslaught of the devil's cast.
However, one man came at last
To Daneland by the grace of God
And set forth in its bloodied sod
To do what not a Dane could do;
Our wisdom failed without renew,
For worthless were the means we tried,
1670 Our weapons and our hands were tied.
We are delivered from our tomb!
The woman who bore in her womb
This child, wherever she may be,
May God bless her eternally,
For God our Father in His will
Gave her this son full bred with skill
To do for us what none could do;
This gift from God she bore is you!
Now Beowulf, most loved of all
1680 On Midgard's grounds, here in my hall
Allow me to call you my son,
To love you for this deed you've done:
A treaty born of peace, I make
Between us. Thus feel free to take
From anything I call my own.
From where I sit atop my throne
My treasure hoard has often spilled
Before those who were not as skilled
And granted gifts from gold to rings,
1690 For deeds accomplished for this king,
Though not a one fought such as you
Against a demon's frothing brew.
Now glory crowns you in its wake
Forever, as you earned its stake
By strength and honor, firmly bound,
For in you, truly, both are found.
May God in all His mercy be
As good to you as before me
And all in Herot He has,
1700 And may your glory never pass!"

Then Beowulf gave his remark:
"We came as Geats in the dark

Intent to heap our heartfelt hands
Upon the dirge, these distant sands
Had cried aloud for in their toil,
To snare the beast polluting soil
And hearth and home; we came to fight
This Grendel with naught but our might.
However, this, my victory,
1710    Has not lain out for you to see
The corpse of Grendel here before
Your presence, strewn across the floor!
My fingers stretched around his fist,
They ripped and tore and turned to twist
His talons loose ere there I stood:
I meant to spill the creature's blood
In here, to hold him in my grip
Till life itself began to slip
Amid the breaking of his heart,
1720    His entrails spewing in the dark
Upon the floor of this great hall,
His lifeless corpse your vision's thrall.
But our Creator had for me
Another plan; the beast pulled free
Though in my lock, I held him bound
The likes no man had ever found,
And freed, he ran in fear's delight,
A fear which gave his value might.
But here above now hangs his claw,
1730    His arm thus rendered, those who saw
The fight know he gave up this prize
And sundered off to his demise.
This freedom cost the beast his will,
And death nipped at each stumbling heel
The while he ran, a panicked fit
Afore his heart then seared and split
Until beneath the monster's chest
His life grew forfeit by behest
Of Hell awaiting in its yawn
1740    The promise of no other dawn.
In tortured suffering, let burn
This devil until God's return
Has yielded judgment's harsh accord,
And Grendel reaps his full reward."
With no more quarrel left in him,
There Unferth's beaming light fell dim
As no more wording meant to chaff
The deeds of Beowulf's old graph

Came forth o'er what he said was done.
1750 For proof enough rose with the sun
As Grendel's arm and claw hung high
Amid the breaking morning sky,
His steely nails appeared to cut
The air in which they swung in rut,
And all had known their make was like
A blade, a knife, an iron pike—
So tough, in fact no mortal's blade
Could dent the flesh; no damage made
Thus rendering the claws in place,
1760 Nor make an end to Grendel's pace,
For none before met these demands
Though one man did with his bare hands.


## 15

Then Hrothgar gave his next decree:
To have his hall cleaned of debris
And met with decoration's flare
Before those guests he hosted there:
His servants, in the hundreds sped
To make the hall as their lord said.
Full tapestries of golden thread
1770 In lofty measure overhead
Appeared to swoon, a joy filled flare
To please those patrons staying there.
But truth be told, the glory beam
Of Herot—its golden gleam—
Had suffered havoc in its shape,
Its hinges seemed to sloop and drape
While hanging, cracked from every slot,
Their hinges bent in every spot;
In fact, the building felt the force
1780 Of meeting Grendel with divorce.
The roof, in fact, stood on its own
Undamaged from the scrape of bone
And flesh involved within the brawl
Erupting in that famous hall
When bloody Grendel made a break,
Though Hell itself would overtake
This monster on his way below
Somewhere beneath the water's tow.
We want to keep our lives intact,
1790 But leaving Midgard is a fact,

For all creations of God's will
Would like to live, but knowing still
We go, we go to where each name
Is written, lost or without blame,
Removing corpses from the place
Where death's cruel grip will fast erase
The living, bringing in its keep
Unbroken peace; an endless sleep
That some call greatest; others least,
1800 Which follows after this life's feast.

Then Hrothgar came and made his way
Unto the hall cleansed of its fray;
The banquet called his heart within,
And gladly bade him enter in.
No celebration held before
In Herot, nor ever more
Would brim with such an adoration
As this one held for the nation
Known as Daneland far abroad.
1810 A mighty host gave thanks to God,
For gathered were the best of men:
The famous, brave, without chagrin
As all along the benches sat
These soldiers licking up the fat
While drinking mead and dousing ale
Amid the brush of song and tale;
The king gave toast to Hrothulf who
Returned it back, the king's nephew
Who raised his cup before the proof
1820 Of Grendel's arm tied to the roof
Of Herot, bereft of harm,
The sentiment secure and warm.
No vast distinction had been made,
Between the king and those who stayed
Amid the merry sport of cheer,
Relinquished of the demon's fear;
No plots composed by Danish kin
Had entered in the hearts of men,
At that time lurking foul and vile
1830 Amidst their present joy-filled smiles.

Within the festive moment's manner,
Hrothgar passed a golden banner
O'er to Beowulf to hold,
His victory spun in its gold,

And placed atop the Geat's head
A helmet jeweled in each thread,
As chiseled mail, the finest made,
Along side of an ancient blade
Became another symbol shared,
1840   Both given to the noble care
Of Beowulf as all who stood
Watched on and gladly understood.

Then Beowulf raised high his glass
To toast the presents made in pass
From Hrothgar's hands unto his own,
Not shamed by boasts, his to condone,
Rewarded greatly before men
Who peered on what it was to win.
No giver of such wealth as these
1850   Four gifts had ever seemed to please
The Geat's heart in warmth's array,
No, not before this very day,
The way it did through Hrothgar's hands.
The helmet's brim held in its bands
The finest steel a man could mold,
Inlaid with gems within each fold,
Yet sturdy made from ridge to rim,
A battle garb to herald him
With much protection, guaranteed;
1860   No sword would dare to make him bleed.

And the king of Danes decreed
A summons for eight of his steeds
To come parade before them all,
Eight steeds then led into his hall
Adorned with golden bridles bound
To every horse, the finest found.
And of the eight, one stood alone,
Befitted in a saddled throne,
A saddle decked with gems and stones
1870   The likes save one had ever known;
Indeed, it had been Hrothgar's seat
Which strode him forth to bring defeat
Unto his foes, this saddle had
Propelled him on to make hearts glad
As where the battle took his men,
He charged on time and time again.
Then Beowulf had seen the glory
Of these gifts that spoke his story,

Honored by what Hrothgar gave,
1880 These weapons that would surely stave
Off conflict's danger, every horse
Consigned to lead the victor's course.
With pride, the king's words seemed to swell
As he bade him to use them well,
These gifts the lord of Daneland's keep
Had placed before the Geat's feet,
Repaying him for braving death;
For taking Grendel's very breath,
Securing freedom for his people,
1890 Purging them from Grendel's evil,
Earning praise and glory's proof
From those who knew this as the truth.

## 16

And more the giver of great rings
Had ordered for his serfs to bring,
Bestowing treasure unto those
Who came to brave the deathly throws
With Beowulf, still at his side,
Those men still living, puffed with pride
Receiving olden armor and
1900 Primeval swords within each hand,
And for the man who slew the beast
Came gold unbound amid their feast.
The demon would have killed again
Had not God sent his chosen man
Who tore the life from Grendel's hide
And managed to turn fate aside.
As then, here now all men must stand
Within their Holy Maker's hands
And move as only He can will.
1910 Our hearts must seek our Maker still.
This world and all its labored days
Bring both the good and evil ways
To every man, this much is clear,
These ways for all abiding here.

The poet's harp began to call
Amid that bright and shining hall
With songs and joyous laughter's mirth
As tales of old were given birth
While gracious Danes drank on and on,

1920    Stretched out across their bench-like thrones.
        Within the words the poet sung,
        He told of Finn, and those who hung
        Betwixt the thread of his command,
        And how he led his sordid band,
        Attacking Hnaf without a word,
        An act that wrought these lyrics heard,
        Destroying half that tribe of Danes
        As then the Jutes took their domain
        And left its king with his fate sealed
1930    Upon that war-torn battlefield.
        Alas, Finn's wife found hatred's blister,
        As she was poor Hnaf's own sister,
        Being taught that fateful day
        What words of faith she heard Finn say
        Bore in their true portent and balm.
        His teething tongue did naught to calm
        Nor soothe her wounds, as two held dear,
        Her brother and her son, to spear
        Fell dead, eloped, entwined with fate.
1940    Her heart could only mourn their state.

        And when the morning sun arose,
        She wept aloud for both of those
        Now taken from her, o'er each one;
        She mourned her brother and her son—
        These two she loved and gave her trust,
        But now they had returned to dust.
        Although the light within these two
        Had faded from its living cue,
        So, too, had all but just a few
1950    Of Finn's regime felt their blood spew,
        Entangled in a massive gore
        With bodies strewn across the floor
        Of battle, Jutes succumbed to death,
        Forever void of living breath.
        So few in fact that not enough
        Remained to seem more than a bluff
        As Hengest, ward of Hnaf's bold troops
        Bade them retreat; let him recoup
        Within the hall where he had stayed,
1960    He and his men, their might displayed.

        From this, King Finn brought his decree:
        A truce to set their warring free
        As words of peaceful method fell.

No victor either side could tell,
When this decree came into bloom.
The hall, and all within its room
Became aware an even split
Between the Danes and Jutes, legit
In every aspect thus designed
1970  King Finn spoke out and thus consigned
Dividing half the hall and throne
unto both sides and making known
This equal measure he would sweep,
A peace both sides there swore to keep.
When gifts at last would pass between
From Finn to Hengest, treasures seen
In form of gold and silver, rings
Among the best, and other things
Deemed worthy of divided spoils.
1980  Each side the richer for their toils,
Then given heavy laden sacks
By halting their prolonged attacks,
Thus warming hearts through gold and gleam,
A comfort forged by treasure's stream.
Both sides in eagerness agreed
To stake their claim for peace's need.
Then Finn divulged his sober oaths;
What wizened men writ down for growth
Of unity, his word and theirs.
1990  With all in order, his affairs
Fell settled in, the one, the other:
Hengest hence forth, like a brother,
Would align himself to live
Affording what Finn chose to give.
Thus neither leader dared to break
Their sacred truce, would not remake
The past amid their current state
Reminding all the Danes to hate
Their new elect, the one who slew
2000  Lord Hnaf within a bloody brew.
No king, no choice the Dane men felt
And thus to Finn, at last they knelt.
But he, in turn, agreed to halt
Those Jutes from pouring pounds of salt
Upon the open wounds, this deal
He made so that the Danes could heal.

A pyre prepared to lay to rest
Lord Hnaf wrought with a frenzied zest

Along with those who went before
2010    This king would burn within the core
Of flame and tune as gold arrived;
They burned, watched by those who survived.
The bloody mail and helmets swore
In death, these men could fight no more,
As soldier toppled soldier's space,
A gruesome sight held at that place.

Then Hnaf's poor sister, Finn's sad wife,
Gave up her son who lost his life
To find his place amidst the flame,
2020    Alike his uncle's charred remains.
Alas, she wept again for them,
And as the flame began to dim,
She sang the psalm meant for the dead,
A solemn praise, then bowed her head.
Amid the smoky hiss and crackle,
Skulls and bones and bloody cackles
Oozed as one; blaze demons ate
Their fleshy prizes bound by fate
Until within the ashy cleft,
2030    Of both sides, there was nothing left.

## 17

Some of his soldiers Finn bade go
To home and lands they longed to know.
But Hengest stayed that winter through,
Awhile within, his hatred grew.
In Daneland lived his every thought—
Though Daneland's shores could not be sought
Because the stormy winter's wrath
Barred them from sailing o'er the path
Across the whale-road's whirling top,
2040    Nor while the frozen waters stopped
The passage from that coast to home,
Until the winter ceased to roam,
Convulsing ocean's waves in knots.
They waited for the new year, hot
With heated rays of sunshine's glare
To come and melt the ice from there,
Inviting earth to bloom and grow,
Yes, Hengest longed for Daneland's glow,
But vengeance placed itself afore

2050 The thought of home, and Hengest swore
The bitter feud would sever yet
For Finn's sword he could not forget.
He schemed and planned and waited, then
Again he schemed until a man
Of Daneland's yolk set in his lap
An ancient blade borne in its flap,
This blade a victory to write,
None other than this *Battle Bright*.
A sword Finn and his men had known,
2060 Had feared before; dreaded its tone,
And would again soon come to know
When Hengest brought its blade to blow.
So, then the Dane rose to his feet
With no intentions of retreat
From what the whispered Danish voice
Provoked within as his new choice.
He plunged the sword edge deep inside
The gut of Finn who aptly died
The likes of beef borne off to slaughter,
2070 Gutted, bled, his life like water
Flowing from his wounded mark,
As every Dane embraced the dark
Remembering how Finn had ruled,
His treachery; the way he fooled.
Thus every Dane within the hall
Rose up in arms and did not stall
Nor hesitate from off the path
Imbued within their scorching wrath
Imparting on the sleeping Jutes
2080 Their hatred in them, absolute,
By way of swords which brought a flood
From bodies strewn, expelling blood
And gore beside their master, Finn,
Whose body, limp, bereft within
Of life, met those beneath his reign.
They took the queen, and in their gain
They looted all her husband had
And loaded up their ship full, glad
And heart felt joy o'er everything.
2090 The loaded gold and gems and rings
As well as necklaces galore,
Then headed for familiar shores
With more than just a vessel full
Of treasure stored within its hull,
For with them willingly she came,

Queen Hildeburh now free of shame
And all her husband's contributions.
She, at last, found retribution
Setting foot on Danish soil,
2100    Thus freed from Finn's corruptive toil.
Aback in Daneland's joyous tone,
Alone no longer on her throne.

The poet finished up his tale;
His audience took gulps of ale
And laughed aloud within the walls
Of Herot, that noble hall.
Those bearing cups came ready bound
With shining cups whose sloshing sounds
Displayed the rhythm born between
2110    The noblemen as dawned their queen,
The sweet Wealhtheow, moving down
The row of benches as her crown
Brought light reflected off the flames
Within the hall to where she came,
Before her husband, Hrothgar, who
Stood by Hrothulf, his brave nephew,
In peaceful measure, seated there,
A friendship yet with weight to bear.
And Unferth sat before the feet
2120    Of Hrothgar making no retreat;
For everyone believed in him,
A brilliant light that would not dim,
Although his kin had felt his blade,
Had seen their blood shed as he bade.
Then Wealhtheow moved looking up,
Gave thanks and spoke: "Accept this cup,
My lord and king! May greatness spread
To you who wears atop his head
The crown afore the Danish folk,
2130    Great giver of his fertile yolk
In form of rings and golden bands!
May here the Geats, from your hands,
Receive great gifts as their reward,
And give them words their acts afford!
The greatest Geat stands before
Your throne, a man your heart adores
As if he were in fact your son.
This great hall stands by what he's done;
Now celebrate his mighty heart,
2140    His courage, as here on your part

While yet a kingdom rests within
Your palm, your people, kith and kin,
All serving you amid their zeal,
Until your death will come and steal
Your kingdom, as death thus shall do.
But know those sons I bore for you
Will have no worries, sheltered by
Your nephew; Hrothulf's watchful eye
Should fate arise and halt your breath,
2150    Yes, your two sons, should you meet death,
Will have protection, for you know
That I, myself, helped Hrothulf grow
When he, himself, was just a boy,
So comfort take within this joy."

As words were ending, came the queen
To see her sons, and one between
Both Hrethric and Hrothmund, whose seats
Were graced by Beowulf's defeat
Of Grendel, still fresh, held within;
2160    The queen sat down beside her men.

## 18

They brought a frothing mug and gave
It to the Geat called "Most Brave,"
Thus Beowulf took in his grip
This gesture born of pure friendship.
And then, a shirt of gleaming mail
Was handed him to thank and hail
His valor, as were golden bands
Along with such a streaming strand
The likes no man had ever seen,
2170    No necklace like this beauty-keen
And shining piece had ere been wrought,
Not since the one brave Hama caught,
The very one the Brosing's owned
That Hama aptly carried home
To be displayed within the gates
Before the city, where his fate
Had etched itself a fine design
Caught in the necklaces refine.
For he had saved not just its wealth,
2180    But likewise, he had saved his health
From treachery within the soul

Of Ermic, who had but one goal:
To slay this hero, ending all
His might, thus make his legend fall,
But still brave Hama came to God
Once he touched on his homeland's sod.
Then Hygelac, the brave grandson
Of Swerting, had the jewel spun
In beauty's splendid appetite;
2190  He swiftly fought in battle might
For all his hands had wrought and won,
But in the end, this came undone
And all he had, this Geat king,
Was lost before the Frisians' sting.
His pride had boasted in its mood
That he should kindle up a feud
With fighters born of Frisia's mark,
But left the Geat in the dark
Without his wealth; without his life,
2200  Thus heaped upon his people strife.
Those precious stones he had procured
Were forfeit to those who endured,
Brought ere upon his ship's broad back
Then lost by his untamed attack;
An enemy that would not yield
Left him to fall beneath his shield.
His body and his coat of mail
Lay broken like a toppled pail,
Spilt out upon the Frankish floor
2210  Where he would rise and war no more.
In this, the Franks stole in his death
That necklace once taking his breath
Plus, everything that shined and sparked
Awaiting fiendish dogs who barked
In triumph as they passed the dead
In rows; the Geats crudely spread
Beside their king, their sanction hooked,
In every place those robbers looked.

The soldiers' roar rose up as smoke.
2220  And then Wealhtheow amply spoke:
"Beloved, dear Beowulf, now wear
These shining jewels, give them care.
Enjoy them with the rings and gold,
Oh, mighty hero, young and bold;
May richer, still, you grow to be,
Let fame and strength come set you free

Awhile they guide your able hand.
And lend these two young men your grand
And noble heart! I will not fail
2230    To ere remember whence you hail
In kindness, nor your blood and sweat.
Your glory I shall not forget.
Forever shall it last hence birth,
Abroad all places on this earth.
May happiness each day ensue,
Good fortune in all you pursue!
Protect the children of my king,
My children with the might you bring!
All men live lives here led in trust,
2240    Protecting Hrothgar as a must,
And fight with much the same degree
As when they raise mugs joyfully.
May what I say move in its task
Your heart to do all that I ask."

She then returned unto her seat.
Around her, many sat to eat.
The savage fate awaiting them
Left not a clue, nor single whim
As nightfall found them tied in thread
2250    As Hrothgar made way to his bed,
And thus his men found sleep's abode.
With little effort, left to goad
His soldiers into deepest sleep.
They stacked the benches in their sweep
Along each row, in blanket's tow,
A head per pillow, dreams to sew.
Alas, their dreams would forfeit breath,
For these drunk fellows slept by death.
Each soldier's shield lay by their head;
2260    Their spears by hand before each bed,
And every heaving chests prevail
Moved up and down in its chain mail.
Such was the custom of the Danes,
Prepared for songs of war's refrain,
No matter if in their homeland
Or off abroad, by his command
Who ruled them, calling them to fight,
They rose and bade their sleep goodnight.
In every instance, all to give;
2270    They knew how soldiers had to live!

Grendel's Mother

## 19

Within the brooding long night's keep,
The warriors sank in deepest sleep.
The payment of that evening's fare
Was much too high for one Dane there
Whose life paid out, as those before
When Grendel frequented the door
Of Herot, within his swell,
Until his crimes sent him to Hell.
Although the news the hall espied,
2280    That such a monster had thus died,
Unknown to them, a monster thrived,
And longed to crush those who survived.
Revenge became her heart's desire,
Female demon's raging fire,
Cold, no comfort from the other,
Lonely, angered, Grendel's mother,
Living in that gloomy lake
Assigned her since Cain's vile mistake,
When he had slain his only brother,
2290    Serving sin, his newfound cover.
Driven out by God's design,
He fled into the desert's shrine,
Thus branded with a murder mark.
And from his heart, there came a dark
And dreary race whose curse rang true,
Inclined to act, to speak and do
The same things as their father did.
So Grendel came to claim his bid,
An outlaw there within the hall,
2300    While waited one to make him fall.
He clawed at Beowulf's brave arm,
Intent to maim; intent to harm,
But, lo, the Geat in that place
Did not forget the saving Grace
Of God, nor all the strength He gave.
And thus he knew the Lord would save
And guide him in his fitful hour.
He slew Grendel by God's power,
Just as God had willed it so.
2310    He tore the fiend, who fled to go
As swiftly as two feet could land
Him duly unto death's cold hand.

His mother's heart hung on her skin
And drove her thus from in her den
Away, the bitter, fitful cringe
Which led her quest born of revenge.

She strode to Herot's design,
Where Danes slept as a coffin's pine,
As if they were already dead;
2320    Her presence bringing only dread,
The end of fortune and good luck
As Grendel's mother's vengeance struck.
No woman, whether battle-bred
Or strong as men, came to their beds
In such a frenzied, fearful fit,
Ensnared and frothing feral spit,
The likes of soldiers caught in heat,
Amidst the battle, no retreat,
While smashing shining, bloody blades
2330    Onto the helmets which displayed
The boar-head emblems, taking in
Their sharpest points without chagrin.
Then soldiers rose in one accord,
Conjoining shields with every sword
While swinging them amid the stench
Of death above each falling bench,
Those benches stacked in awkward piles,
There causing men to fail their styles,
Thus leaving mail and helmets, too,
2340    Upon the ground amid the cue
Of terror taking, shaking hold
As horror let her forms unfold.

Aware the men knew she was there
Made evil move with hastened care,
And thus to save her life she took
But just one man within her hook,
Then fled in haste, her vengeance met.
One man alone with her regret
Would meet her quota's appetite,
2350    And thus she ran into the night
Unto the moors, her meal intact,
Not one time glancing o'er her back.
The hostage in the demon's claw
Had been a hero, much he saw
In all the years he stood beside
King Hrothgar, held within his pride

As one the king so dearly loved,
His closest friend now in the glove
Of death, now slain amid the strife
2360    Of she who came and took his life.

No Geat could have barred her way.
Indeed, their prince had gone to stay
Along with them in better beds,
Thus Beowulf had lain his head
On different pillows; different rooms
Than this one now conceived in gloom.
While Herot burst into shouts,
The mother demon raged about
And in her manner took the arm
2370    Of Grendel, who once gave great harm
To Herot, as many saw;
Indeed, she left there with his claw.
Alas, the saddened heartfelt sieve
Had once again bade Daneland grieve,
And neither side of beast nor men
Appeared to have the total win!

The wise old king, in fear and grief,
Met anger's summons, no relief
Within his heart confined in dread
2380    For his best loved of friends was dead.
At once the messenger released
Made haste, his lord's will thus appeased.
To Beowulf he made his way,
The saddened news he had to say
Brought Beowulf and all he led
To see the king o'er what was said.

The dawn broke through, but darkness reigned
As Hrothgar cried to God in pain
And asked Him "Will this sorrow end?"
2390    Then many Geats traipsed the bend
With footstep's echo in the hall,
Eloping silence in each fall.
The best of fighters here or there
Found Hrothgar sulking in his chair,
That gray-haired chieftain wondering
If God would halt the monster's sting.

Rehearsed in prose, the Geat prince
Found words to drop in ordered sense,

Thus ordered were each thought he'd say,
2400 Inquiring of that night's long stay;
The Dane's great lord met word's release,
As Beowulf inquired of peace
Within the hall by every Dane,
And if the night had held no pain.

## 20

Then Hrothgar moaned a muffled breech
With shifting sadness in his speech:
"No happiness, so do not ask!
We Danes are drinking fury's flask.
My loved and noble friend is dead,
2410 My friend who fought beside each thread
Of battle woven war torn yield,
Beside me on each battlefield,
Aeschere, whom I speak of now
Is gone, no more to answer how
Or when or why in counsel's care.
Thus snatched and taken by his hair,
This Yrmenlaf's instructor and
His eldest brother, noble, grand,
Yes gone, no more to stand beside
2420 And keep me fit amidst my stride.
If only all were such as he,
Those soldiers who come openly
To serve my will, my life to save;
Alas, not one can be as brave!
Another fiend has found us here
And taken one I held so dear
Within her chomping, crunching grip,
A feast for her along her trip—
And who knows where the beast might be,
2430 Her belly full capacity?
For Grendel's death, she has arrived
With vengeance brewing, she has strived
To punish me for your avail,
Dear Beowulf, that you had failed!
But no, the deaths at Grendel's hand
Were too much for my precious land;
Arriving here but in a day
The beast of death you came to slay
Had fled, his bloody corpse withdrawn
2440 As his arm was the sun at dawn,

But now another like the first
Has come again, my hall thus cursed—
Or so it has to surely seem
To those who hoped to lay and dream,
Instead to find that noble brand
Of hero dead by demon hands,
For all who new Aeschere's name
Will miss the giving death made tame.
My people, peasants long endeared
2450    To spending days at work, appeared
Before my sentries stating claims
Of two foul creatures without names,
Two monsters in the moors and marsh
Whose features were both cruel and harsh,
Those giant beings living where
The deserts winds burst through the air.
My wise men heard a further tale,
That one beast seen had been female.
The other, like a man, but more
2460    In strength, they spread as truthful lore.
All scared, afraid, they fled to see
If they could gain some aid from me
In Herot, their hopeful flame.
Then Grendel they chose as the name
Of he who walked and stalked the mire,
The burning hearts like torch's fire:
None could say who fathered him,
Or if more lurked the likes of them,
These two brash fiends who haunted all,
2470    Those peoples fleeing to my hall.
Such evil hidden under riffs,
Beneath large stones or under cliffs
Where mists and streams in darkened caves
The likes of these would clam and crave,
Where waters froze, and snakelike roots
Sought shelter, joining to pollute
This ancient lake, thus hit their mark
By keeping all its waters dark.
At night, like flames amid the tip
2480    Of torches held within the grip
Above the surface of the lake
Brought fear to those before its wake.
This very lake, nobody knows
Its heart nor just how far it goes
Below its surface, no man's mind
Can speak such answers, cannot find

The wisdom of its virile keep,
Just nightmares granted in their sleep.
A deer or stag run down by hounds
2490   Would rather stop before the grounds
Astride the water's edge and die
Than chance to dive within its sty.
It isn't far, this water's edge,
But in its form, a frightful pledge
Has kept us all within its thrall!
Here as I speak from in my hall,
When winds abroad stir underneath
The brooding storm kept in the sheath
Of darkened clouds, as black as rain
2500   Disposing of the heavens' pain
The color makes its final plea,
That dreaded lake we all must see.
Again, our only surest aid
Will come from you, who unafraid
Defeated Grendel face to face.
Now hidden in some dank, dark place
Lurks Grendel's mother, should you dare,
Go forth and seek her dismal lair!
Again, save us and as before
2510   Your treasure will grow more and more
With ancient gems and stones and gold;
So, let your victory unfold!"

## 21

Then Beowulf unloosed his throat
To speak of winning, dare the moat:
"Your sorrow now is at an end!
I will avenge your martyred friend,
Lest you sit here in gloom's parade,
No, mourning debts are duly paid.
Each human living reaches death,
2520   The first breath drawn to his last breath;
Thus he who can should make a name.
For death can bring the greatest fame,
The wonders of this splendid goal
Will satisfy the very soul.
Arise, great king of this great land,
And let me lend again my hand,
For time is not for us to squander,
Thus let's find this lady monster.

Here, I promise you, my lord
2530    She'll taste the wrath of my broad sword.
This fiend will have my fist to grind,
No shelter, safety, hole to bind
Her body in, no tree to scale,
Nor lake to dive beneath, her wail
Will be enough as by your side
I say her sins she cannot hide.
Just bear in patience one more day
This misery here on display;
You'll see between us two the stronger,
2540    One day more, I ask no longer."

Then the old king leapt in joy,
Gave thanks to God for His employ,
As Beowulf had words of strength,
Assuring victory's full length.

Then Hrothgar called his men to course,
And thus they offered him his horse,
Full bridled, saddle placed in gear.
A sight, which gave the people cheer,
For nothing matched their great king's stride
2550    Atop his steed; a splendid ride;
The high-shield wielding soldiers stayed
In line with Hrothgar as they bayed
And marched into the lands unknown
By many, going for his throne.

In search of seeds she might have sewn,
The monster's steps before them shone
Like sunlight in the noon of day
And took them through the forest's way.
2560    They followed each her heavy foot
Across the barren, gloomy soot
Unto the marshes' shadowed ground,
Her burden was the body bound
Within her clutches, weighing down
Her footfall as the bloody crown
Of Hrothgar's best and dearest friend
Lay cracked and cropped, no more to mend.

Her trail forced them to shift and swerve
As they ascended hilly curves
2570    Which hosted rocky, jutting steeps
That barely held their feet in keep,

And over narrow, winding paths,
Incumbent with the demon's wrath,
And down again where creatures lurk,
While slipping, sliding in each jerk,
Until they neared their final goal,
And found the monster's gruesome hole.

In front, brave Hrothgar urged his horse,
An action done without remorse
2580    While taking those whose tracking skills
Were of his best, thus making nil
The chance they wouldn't find their way.
Abruptly, trees began to sway
While arching down in clumpy rows
Across the dampest stones in tow,
Those grayest stones in dismal rot
Where wood and wind, it seemed, begot
The notion of a demon's wake.
Below them lurked a brooding lake,
2590    Its water, red, a bloody brew
Amid the boiling, frothy hue.
The bodies of the Danish men
Began to shiver from within,
Those warriors with no relief
Became tormented, racked with grief,
When every eye beheld the slaughter,
There above that steaming water,
Catching sight the bloody red
Of poor Aeschere's severed head.
2600    Then from its hold, their eyes returned
Unto the water as it burned
And steamed in frothy, putrid gore,
Then swirled and swished upon the shore.

The sounds of battle horns rang out,
Then rang again their final shout.
The fighters' weapons found their place,
Removed and settled in the space
Before the jaunting water's edge.
Within the murky, dismal sledge
2610    The men beheld atop the lake
A host of teething, seething snakes,
Amazing serpents tossed in coil,
There wrapped within the water's boil,
Such beastly creatures, cruel in stock
Stretched out atop the dismal rocks—

The sort of beasts that openly
Assail those who break out to sea
Within the early break of dawn,
Caught taught within their mouthy brawn.
2620    The sounds of horns brought from the lush
And blaring noise a hastened rush
As angrily the creatures fled,
Convulsing at this coming dread.
Amid their flight, an arrow aimed
By Beowulf set loose and maimed
A rugged beast, slow to depart,
As lo, the arrow pierced its heart;
Its lifeblood ebbed unto the murk
As death grabbed hold within its jerk
2630    And writhed and wrangled in the beast.
Before its final breath released,
The fighters caught it by the nape
Before it could make its escape
By anchoring their boar-curved spears,
And pulled amid their soldiers' cheers,
Until it reached the rocky shore,
Pulled up the bluff while leaking gore.
Then all agape and wonder struck
Gazed at the creature from the muck,
2640    This great endeavor, horror's wail,
Embodied in the strangest scales.

Then Beowulf took up his arms,
Not fearing what could bring him harm,
Full knowing fear would not prevail,
And did not lend to placing mail
Abroad his chest, but new the truth,
That mail could save him from the proof
Of monsters snatching at his heart,
And would uphold his willing part,
2650    Thus meeting who he must in fight
To take the wrongs and make them right.

The helmet Hrothgar gave to him
Would block cruel teeth amid his swim;
That treasure lined in shining mirth
Would span abroad his head in girth,
That very one so finely wrought
With metal hammered firm and taut
By ancient hands of metal craft,
Those ancient smiths whose pleasured draft

2660   Had shifted o'er, a silent rattle,
       Goading others' blades in battle,
       Knowing theirs could not withstand
       This one held in the Geat's hand.
       So when he swum beneath the brood,
       He would maintain his current mood,
       And reach the water's deep command,
       Thus safely touching its dark sands.

       And Unferth aided to his hunting,
       Gave a fine blade known as *Hrunting*;
2670   Such an ancient, well renowned
       Embodied blade came well endowed
       In make and mold, its iron edge
       Stood boldly in its gruesome pledge
       To act in battle as designed.
       Its shining, rune-laid blade, refined
       By rustic colors meshed and twined
       Allayed and pinned, compressed and lined
       By way of blood left through the years,
       Spoke freely of its cleaving cheers.
2680   Not one who swung its mighty form
       In conflict saw its raging storm
       And felt the pangs of their defeat.
       None wielding ever made retreat,
       For *Hrunting* drove its foes to death,
       And did so seeming to have breath;
       Alive and full within the hands
       Of whosoever gave command—
       And Beowulf was not the first
       To bring this blade unto the worst—
2690   Unto the camps of fighting foes,
       Or in the trust it would bestow
       A victory for honor's theme,
       Fulfilling every hero's dream.
       This gesture lent on Unferth's part
       Was meant to bring a brand-new start
       To Beowulf's and his beginning,
       That first time when drunken grinning
       Brought a mouthful's snapping host
       Amidst the words of Unferth's boast.
2700   And though he held a soldier's rank,
       He passed the sword before that bank
       Where Beowulf and he exchanged
       Its hilt, the better of them ranged
       And ready, his to undertake

The mission there beneath that lake.
No, Unferth feared the depths below
And gave up glory; would not go
Thus forfeiting eternal fame,
Not bringing grandeur to his name.
2710 But Beowulf held no alarm;
He readily dove into harm.


## 22

Then brave Ecgtheow's bold son broke
The silent air and staunchly spoke:
"Remember, king, all we have shared,
Those kindred words of love ensnared
Within your heart as now I go
To death, perhaps, I do not know.
But should I die, oh gracious king,
Then comfort now your words will bring,
2720 For all I ask in my demand
Is that you lead those I command,
Protecting them by what was said,
Should I, their leader, end up dead.
As well, the gifts you gave to me,
Dear friend, please send them openly
In love to Hygelac, my kin,
The Geat Lord, so that again
He may, with all, see golden light,
Thus knowing you are one of might;
2730 That Daneland's lord is great and proud,
And loved me as a son endowed
With every gift a father shares,
Though should I enter in death's snares,
Those gifts I claimed the while I stayed
In your care will be thus displayed.
And now to you, Unferth, I say
In your hands here my sword will stay,
My battle-worn, companion's hilt
Shall rest with you, not bearing guilt
2740 For what has passed between us two,
Take hold and know my words are true:
With *Hrunting's* blade I'll carve and mold
My glory, left in legends told,
My name remembered for my worth,
Or death shall sweep me from this earth!"

His tongue grew calm, and not a sound
Came more as he leapt from the ground
into the frothing horror's wake
Beneath the surface of the lake,
2750    Awaiting none to answer him,
He sank until his form grew dim.
Below the waves, he dropped and dove
For many hours, then a cove
Of muddy soil caught in his sight,
And readied him for peril's plight.

Then she, the demon of the deep,
Who for a hundred half year's keep
Had governed waters underneath
The seething lake top's bloody wreath,
2760    Discovered someone from the plane
Above her watery domain
Eclipsed her land of all things wet,
And seemed potentially a threat.
The she-wolf surged her wretched claws
And groped the hero in her paws,
But each attempt to scratch and rip
Fell short within her horrid grip,
And nothing offered from her nails
Could break through Beowulf's ring mail.

2770    The demon mother bore him full,
His armor, sword, and all in pull,
Unto her home; the hero tried
To free his weapon from his side,
But all attempts were met in vain.
Their struggle in that dark domain
Brought other creatures from the deep
To see what she held within her keep,
A horrid hive of villainy
Who tore with teeth consistently,
2780    Along with razor tusks that stabbed
Into his mail shirt, poked and jabbed
Along their way to watch him drown,
As he went ever further down.

Then suddenly he realized
He hadn't met with his demise,
And, lo, the witch of water deep
Had dropped him in some ancient keep,
Some long forgotten battle hall

Whose roof kept him from water fall,
2790   No liquid heat, nor creature hosts
Could touch him there beneath the coast,
For where he stood kept water out,
Within this building, standing stout.

A burning aura brightly shone
To light the path of the unknown,
The lake appeared to be such light,
And effervesced a blazing sight.
Within the brilliance of the glow,
The path then seemed one he must know,
2800   For there he saw in her abode
The cusp of evil's foulest node,
The water wench in her full shape,
And knew there would be no escape.

He thrust his battle-ready blade
Into her head, a sight relayed
By echoes of the iron tune
Which hissed as glimmered every rune
In eloquence etched on the sword,
But nothing brought in his accord
2810   Of strength and might offered her harm,
For like her son, her skin held charm
And providence o'er earthly make
Of any weapon, staff or stake.
Thus Beowulf came to decide
That having *Hrunting* on his side
Meant little in his current state,
And left the sword to find its fate
In other hands, for now it failed,
This weapon once so highly hailed.
2820   They tossed the while each other gripped,
Then she, the demon, tore and ripped
With anger's potent ransom spurned,
Her claws lashed out as round they turned.
Her teeth gnashed holes on every side
Of what had been King Hrothgar's pride—
The helmet given as a sign
To Beowulf now lost its shine,
No other time before to lose
In battle, but it was no use
2830   To he that wore it now before
The demon-beast that ripped and tore.

But Beowulf wished to endure;
The chance to prove his might, secure
In battle-ready, promised flare,
Awaiting glory promised there.
His anger tossed the blade aside,
That rune-filled emblem's clanging tide
An echo on the floor beneath,
As it had given no relief.
2840   His hands, he deemed, would speak the truth;
His fingers tightened would bare proof
That he held no need of a weapon,
His strength needed no deception.
Glory comes to those whose goal
To win burns in their very soul!
No fear, and ever growing bolder,
Beowulf reached for her shoulder,
Spurned by anger's prudent bite,
His strength increased to his delight
2850   And thus he was the first to score
By slamming her onto the floor.
Within the rush, her body slumped
As in his heart, the blood that pumped
Surged wilder than it had before,
And as she lay there on the floor,
The boldest of the Geat brand
Prepared to pounce her, lest she stand.

But Grendel's mother held her own,
2860   Prepared to make her presence known,
Exacting claw and nail per swing,
Her fervor, raw, intent to bring
The harm and fall of he who came
To earn himself forever fame.
His tiresome steps brought body aches,
That best of fighter's shaky quakes
Intent to fell the mighty one.
And as fatigue's last bout was done,
The demon-queen shrieked in her lunge,
2870   Exploding in her dismal grunge,
And landed heavily her shape
Upon the fighter as a drape
That drops from rings and rods to quell
A dying hero's final yell.
Thus Beowulf could only lay,
For she had pinned his strength at bay.
A frothing mouth of heinous teeth

Gave grinning glee amid relief,
For there, the demon did not stagger,
2880    Calling forth her brown-stained dagger,
Dried with blood from victims past,
And readied to exact its blast
Avenging Grendel, her dead son,
The payback given to this one
She now held down, intent to maim
Until his form death's call would claim.

But once again, his mail prevailed
And locked the blade the wench assailed
And sought to dive within the chest
2890    Of Beowulf, but o'er his breast
The clanging sound of rusty steel
Brought forth relief, renewing zeal
For had no mail secured that space,
Then death would have stood in its place.
Brave Ecgtheow's bold son, in turn,
In diving deep, a witch to spurn,
Would have arrived upon death's shore,
Had not the mail turned back the sore
Intended to destroy his life
2900    By way of that old, blood-caked knife,
And more so, Holy God's refine
To lavish victory's design.

The Lord of Heaven granted might;
His judgment for all truth and right
The second Beowulf could stand
And ready make his ample hands.

## 23

Renewed within his nagging plight,
A hopeful beacon caught his sight
Upon the wall, a joy-filled pang,
2910    Illumined in its lofty hang,
A treasure hoard not made of gold,
No, one meant for his hands to hold,
As there an ancient blade, reliant,
Crafted by some long dead giant
Full of decorated strength.
So massive in its rune-filled length,

That not an average man could lift
Its weighted pose, lay claim its gift.

But Beowulf did not befit
2920  The standard man, nor did he quit.
Thus from its hanging sheath's repose,
He snapped the chain around its nose,
The hilt, unleashing savage rage,
Now fevered; angry to engage,
Arising in its massive dread
Atop the soldier's war-scarred head
And forced a blow, his final check,
Thus catching her across her neck,
Dismembering the whole way through
2930  Her head, her bones, her taught sinews.
The she-wolf's body, lifeless, fell
Unto the floor, her soul to Hell,
As bloody, wet and dripping gore,
The blade had sent her to the floor,
And Beowulf rejoiced before
Her lifeless form upon the floor.

No sooner than this deed was done,
A brilliant light much like the sun
Illumined darkness in her fall,
2940  And brightly lit that ancient hall.
He followed there along the wall,
In answer to his anger's call,
A tight, firm hold upon that blade;
There was a debt yet to be paid.
He hunted Grendel, long since dead,
Intent to take the vile beast's head
As final payment for his deeds,
For every Dane the beast made bleed,
The slaughter of those sleeping men,
2950  For coming time and time again
To Herot, Hrothgar's keep
While soldiers nestled in their sleep.
This for the ones, fifteen or more,
Who Grendel ate and smashed their gore
Upon the walls, or on his way
Through murky moors with more to slay,
A dinner snack within his grip.
But Beowulf would end his trip
By taking final vengeful right,
2960  Repaying Grendel bite for bite,

And lo, he found the villain slain,
His armless corpse, no life retained,
His armless form the one had made
In Herot, his might displayed,
Yet now that monster lay there, dead,
And Beowulf's sword took his head.

Awhile above, the water boiled,
Thus seething, hissing as it toiled
Made full of blood upon its waves,
2970    And men assumed the dismal grave
Gave Beowulf no sign of hope,
Those gray-haired men who sought the slope
And peered into the water's edge,
With Hrothgar, thought the final pledge
Of Beowulf would go unsung.
Each patron kept their head down hung
While speaking of the fighter's might,
And how he had succumbed to plight
Within the grip of demon death,
2980    And surely offered his last breath.
With heavy hearts, the men went home,
Those Danes whose faith began to roam,
And even Hrothgar's hope was spun,
So with the heated noonday sun,
He left with them, his Danes eloped,
While stayed the Geats there and hoped
Beyond all hope their vision spied
Their famous lord; he had not died,
For they refused belief, these men,
2990    That they would not see him again.

Below the waves where death was dealt,
The ancient blade began to melt
As much the same as dripping ice
Eternal God, in His device,
Sets loose as only He can do,
The Ruler of the old and new,
The Crafter of the wind and sod,
The One and only Living God.

Though treasure bound in all delight
3000    With every bit of wealth in sight,
It came by Beowulf's command
That only two things touched his hands:
The head of Grendel, limp as silt,

Aside the giant's crested hilt;
The rest had all dissolved to mud
By way of Grendel's boiling blood.

Then swam the battle-weary soul,
Whose victory achieved his goal,
Away from death beneath the brew
3010    Where lifeless monsters totaled two;
Came swimming now in water's clean
And calm, no evil left to glean,
For peace erupted o'er the lake
Where once reigned evil in its wake.
But now the silent joy was spread
For those corrupt, vile beasts lay dead.

That noble lord o'er land and sea
Came bearing joyful his decree
In shape and form of burdens' weight,
3020    A winning tale, his to relate.
His Geat crew rekindled joy
As their eyes held in full employ
The image of the mighty thane,
The one who came to aid the Danes,
And there to God, they all gave thanks
For greeting safely on those banks
The man they all gripped with their arms,
Before them now, away from harm;
Together, they departed, all
3030    Determined to reach Hrothgar's hall.

The grateful Geats gladly bore
The helmet and the mail he wore
While at their backs, the water filled
With thickened blood the monster spilled.

They paced themselves; they quickly strode
In merriment across those roads,
Remembering the path, inclined,
As soon the lake grew far behind
Those hero-happy Geat men
3040    Whose faces wore each one a grin.
Though doing so beneath the load
Of Grendel's massive skull to goad,
The weight requiring four to steer—
Its form imbued upon a spear—
Yet joyfully its gruesome mirth

They gladly bore amid their girth,
Unwavering beneath its pain,
Intent for every single Dane
To see it, held within its thrall
3050    As they approached that gold-trimmed hall.

Then fourteen Geats and their lord
Set forth in triumphant accord
Upon the grassy meadow down
To seek the man of Daneland's crown.

To Herot, the bold prince strode,
Full garbed inside Hrothgar's abode.
His battle-manner told the story,
His the trappings sewn in glory,
Seeking counsel with the one
3060    Whose orders now at last were done,
Saluting Hrothgar as he sped
In haste to bring him Grendel's head.

Then Beowulf wound in his flare
The rancid tentacle-like hair
Of Grendel's mane, and brought it where
The Danes all sat before him there
Immersed in drink, their queen stood by
As such a sight caught every eye.
Indeed, though odd, not one despaired;
3070    The warriors all stopped and stared.

## 24

The Geat prince afforded speech,
This Beowulf, proud of his breech:
"Behold, great king and Healfdane's son,
The symbol of my duty done,
Victoriously, here I stand,
Brought by my noble Geat band.
To offer this, I drew near death;
I almost offered my last breath
Beneath the water: surely, dead
3080    I would have been, and had no head
To boldly bear, the demon queen
The victor, and my death unseen,
If not for God, our Father, Who
From Heaven saw my actions through.

Not even *Hrunting*'s mighty blade
Could offer hope, though Unferth bade
Me use it for that noble cause.
It left me stripped before death's jaws,
Though I, myself, to no avail,
3090    It seemed, brave king, would thus prevail,
But then the Ruler of all men
So granted me a chance to win,
For there He showed me on the wall
What words cannot depict at all,
A wonder, beauty shining bold,
An ancient sword locked in its hold.
Thus God gives aid when man is lost,
When into danger, man is tossed,
And nothing, nor no mortal man
3100    Can do the things our Father can.
I used what He had shown to me,
Drew forth its blade, swung mightily
When He secured my chance to feast
In victory o'er that foul beast.
That rune-marked blade then burned away,
Though once the fire held its stay,
For bloody, boiling oozing sludge
From in the beast kept fast its grudge
And bade the giant's weapon gone,
3110    With just the hilt left to be shone.
The sins of crime and murdered Danes
Have been avenged, oh noble thane
And lord of all in Daneland's fold.
I promise, whether young or old,
The brave and weak, the women, too,
Your soldiers, king, and even you,
Will find rejoicing in this keep
And nevermore fear while you sleep.
No, none in Herot shall fear
3120    Their rest, great lord; death is not here,
For not a beast, mother or son,
Will come, the victory is won."

At this, the golden sword hilt made
In manners of an ancient trade
Passed o'er to Hrothgar's wrinkled grip,
And he then pondered on its trip
From demon dens and monster's hands;
This weapon now his to command,
An ancient relic shaped in might

3130    By gifted craftsman gone from sight.
Thus Grendel and who gave him birth
Had both been driven from the earth,
And nothing more of them was said,
With God's foul enemies now dead.
That ancient hilt came thus to be
In Hrothgar's care, a fine decree
Expressing his majority
As Daneland's best authority.

That elder king then bent his head
3140    Close to the hilt, for runes down tread
Its layout, and the story read
Exposed those ancient warring threads
Of good and evil, dust and mud
Swept up amid the one great flood
As open skies burst in their sway
And washed the giants all away,
Which brought on suffering and pain
The while they walked the Lord's domain,
And how they died at His command,
3150    Receiving judgment from His hands,
Emphatic water where they fled
Found those who hated God all dead.

Then Hrothgar read more letter runes
Which he found cut within the dunes
And slats amid that shining hilt,
Which shone for whom that sword was built;
The very name the runes displayed
Explained for whom the sword was made,
With every fine detail inlaid:
3160    Its twisted handle without blade
And ornate carvings in its make
Beholding images of snakes.

With every ear intently full,
The son of Healfdane surged his pull,
And thus the hall in silence hung
As he at once unleashed his tongue.
"Before you all, here what I say
I say from my long-lasting stay
As master o'er the mighty Danes,
3170    Long seeking right in their domains:
That in this world's unnumbered span,
There never was a better man

Than Beowulf, that Geat prince!
None here could ever dare convince
Me otherwise, for at your name,
The world abroad knows of your fame,
My friend and son, yes, all abroad,
Your name is known where ere you trod.
So hold this knowledge in your heart,
3180    And keep a wise frame ere you start,
For you are patient in your strength,
And went for us the extra length
Before the beasts, as we are weak,
And thus before you now I speak.
My vow, my words are good as gold,
And I will do what I have told
You thus I would, our friendly bond,
A vow from which I shan't abscond.
Your might will scour any evil,
3190    Thus you will protect your people
Here, and on, no longer these
In Daneland, now up off their knees.
Be not the man that Heremod was;
His ego overstepped the cause
Of those, my people, bringing down
Destruction to the Danish crown.
His fevered wrath slew any able—
He, and those who at his table
Dined with him unknowingly
3200    Until too late, bore death's decree.
When all alone, in his employ
Were none of life's implicit joys,
Such as the sharing with one's kin,
Nor such companionship with men
As we have known. His lust for blood
Corrupted all within its flood,
Though God above gave him the will
To triumph in fantastic skill,
But, lo, his evil, twisted spirit
3210    Drew destruction ever near it.
Nothing shared from in the hoards
Of treasures kept could ere afford
His soldier's knowledge through his name,
Nor guide them on their road to fame.
No, only anguish, hurt and pain
Did he bear forth for every Dane.
Take heed in this, his lesson taught,
The means with which these words were sought

And know the virtues of a king:
3220 I am but one with such to bring
As now an aged and elder sort
Who tells you this to lend support
And guide you on your growing way,
Yes, for you, all of this I say.
Eternal God, our Lord above,
Grants some men wisdom, others love,
Some gather knowledge, others wealth,
As others have their life-long health,
And some He gives a steady fate,
3230 While others, yet, He still makes great.
This earth is God's, and in His heart,
He chooses on some to impart
The broadest lands, the greatest fame,
On others, He builds up their name,
While others, still, His riches flow
And wealth and wisdom He bestows—
For who in mortal sense, unwise,
Will contemplate his own demise
While living in the prime of life,
3240 Not caring for his coming strife?
Affluence in his every turn
Abides with what he cannot learn:
No troubles, age, or crude disease
Afflict him; bring him to his knees,
No warring cry of nations sparred,
Nor winning spoils from him are barred,
For all the earth at his word spins.
How does he know when he has sins?"


## 25


"But pride creeps in, then sinks its teeth,
3250 And though the time it takes is brief,
It grows and nourishes its hold,
Eliciting its crafty mold.
And while the watcher of his soul
Remains asleep without control,
A slayer of the just draws near,
His clutches on the feral fear
Amid the bow intent to harrow
With his taught and dreadful arrows.
In his chest, their iron tips
3260 Take hold, beneath his helmet, slip

Until the light elopes the dark,
And every arrow hits its mark.
A helpless fool devoid of purging
He becomes. The Dark One's urgings
Gash his flesh, for without health,
He soon forgets he clung to wealth
Within the world, his clawing fit
To hold onto the whole of it,
No glory, nor no honor found
3270    In anything he once was bound,
Not giving from his ring-hoard's lot.
It seems to be how he forgot
The measure of his fated worth,
That glory God gave him at birth,
Thus in forgetting, did not care.
And when his body fails from wear,
His flesh and bones, by God's own hand,
Will wither at the Lord's command.
Then yet another will arrive
3280    And take his gold, this soul, alive,
In Heaven's care, intent to live,
And from his treasure hoard, to give
From every relic, new or old,
Not giving greed its lusty hold.
Beware this evil wickedness,
Great Beowulf, all I profess
Before you, wonder of all men
Is meant to guide your path from sin,
So choose eternal, joyful bliss,
3290    That in this life you will not miss
The truth of what I here confide,
Thus push away from foolish pride!
Your health and fame are only here
But for a brief encounter; fear
Has not set in, no doubting whim.
But soon enough, the both of them
Must be returned to where they came,
The end of health; the end of fame,
For some disease, perhaps a sword
3300    Whose edge will bring you to the Lord,
Or yet a fire will consume
Your life upon the spinning loom,
Then still, a spear set forth in flight
Will bring you down, great man of might,
Or even waves, those you have calmed,

Will hence entomb and thus embalm
Your form with salty water's rife,
And yet you might meet with a knife,
Or worse, the terror of old age,
3310    When darkness creeps across life's stage.
Yes, Death, the swift avenger's fit
Shall come; there's no escaping it.
A hundred half-years, I have led
The Danes; have laughed, and cried, and bled
Protecting them in all their worth
From many peoples of this earth,
My sword and spear within my grip,
Such that our footing would not slip
And not a soul, no, not a one
3320    Beneath the span of God's high sun
Dared wage a war or lift a hand
Upon my most beloved Daneland.
But, lo, reversal came to me
When Grendel sought us openly,
Invading Herot to dine
On people that I claimed as mine;
My sorrow burst upon the moor,
Ere Grendel rushed on through my door,
For nothing seemed to lift me up.
3330    Then thanks to God, I raise my cup:
You came, and slew my misery,
You took the grief from deep in me,
And as it ended, here I live,
Now peering o'er this gift you give;
Yea, in these very words I've said,
Behold we all the demon's head!
Go in, brave prince; come, let us feast,
For you have rid us of the beast.
And thus I say come find your seat
3340    And fill your gut with what's to eat,
For this is what your fame rewards;
Come feast upon my treasure hoard;
My treasure by the break of dawn
We both shall share here at my throne."

The Geat did as Hrothgar bade,
That gray and wise king who displayed
His jubilation as was able,
Beowulf thus found his table
And the feast began again
3350    Amid those many mighty men.

The Danes, the Geats, both united
For the time in peace provided
By the hero o'er them all,
Those famous fighters in that hall.

Within the frame of ale's delight,
The darkened sky called forth the night.
The men arose; King Hrothgar, too,
That gray-haired king bade them adieu,
And left them in their merry keep
3360      For his eyes beckoned him to sleep.

And Beowulf, now amply fed,
Was glad there was a waiting bed
As rest collided with his frame,
Worn out from earning his great fame.
A Danish soldier took the load
Of houseguest and showed him the road
Which led him down the quiet path
Away from noise and violent wrath,
3370      Where sleep could cover he and those
Who followed him; the one's who chose
The chance to go where ere he led;
Now sleep would claim each in his bed;
These Geats garbed in Hrothgar's care
Were want for naught while resting there,
For any want or need expressed,
The king assured was finely dressed.
Then Beowulf embraced his nest;
That hall, much better than the rest,
3380      Rose high above his sleeping head
While he found peace within his bed,
While Herot shone in the night,
A golden symbol for the right;
The Geats slept until the song
Of some black raven came along,
Exalting its ambitious tune,
Which chased away the silver moon;
His happy song brought Heaven's halo,
Burning off night's dreary shadow.

3390      Those wave-riders rose from bed,
Ambitious for the open tread
Of salty seas, intent to roam
Until their voyage brought them home,

Indeed, their hearts were fast on track,
Daydreaming of their vessel's back.

Then Unferth gave his well-famed sword,
That *Hrunting*, in the same accord
As he had done before the lake
To Beowulf, his thus to take,
3400    And asked him to accept this prize.
The prince did so with gleaming eyes
And so declared the blade unique;
Well formed to serve his own physique.
His words laid not a single blame
Upon the sword, indeed his fame
Did not enlarge his mighty head,
And thus a hero's words he said!
The Geats garbed and fully armed
Were ready, for their thoughts now charmed
3410    Their anxious hearts, soon to be gone.
In haste, the prince sought Hrothgar's throne,
Where sitting, lo, the great lord dwelled,
Abiding Beowulf's farewell.

## 26

Then from the wells of silence broke
The words of Beowulf, who spoke:
"We strode the whale-road to arrive
Upon these shores, intent to thrive
And conquer where our feet would roam,
But now we must return back home,
3420    Our ship decks full of golden stacks
To bring our lord, King Hygelac.
But Daneland was a giving host;
You welcomed us unto your coast
In manners warm, with duty's care,
You've rendered more than your fare share.
Just know, great king, my word holds worth-
That anything upon this earth
Your heart desires needing done,
Send forth for me, and like your son
3430    To earn more love from in your heart,
I'll come and fully do my part,
If that is more than what I've done,
Yes, call and see that battle won.
Should word depart from shore to shore,

And I hear of those leaning war
Upon your back; oppressing you,
Then there is nothing I won't do,
For warriors, a thousand score,
Will come to Herot's own door,
3440    A thousand Geats fully armed
To see your throne is never harmed.
My trust I place in Hygelac:
Though he is young, he would attack
On your behalf, if I but asked,
No need disguising honor, masked
No longer, for as I am here,
Not only would you have my spear,
But every Geats' war-torn gear,
Yes, every single Geat spear,
3450    To shield and honor as we serve,
For this, great king, you thus deserve,
And certain as my face you see,
Know Hygelac would stand by me.
And one day, should your eldest son,
Bold Hrethric, sail beneath our sun,
His welcome in the Geat court
Would be the friendliest of sport.
For no one setting foot on sand
Whose travels from a far-off land
3460    Have brought them thus in nothing less
Will find but friendship, I confess,
If virtue be their soldier's brand,
Then they will clasp a welcome hand."

At this, before those friendships tied,
King Hrothgar aptly thus replied:
"All-knowing God has moved your tongue;
Before Him, now my head is hung,
For nothing said so bold and wise
Has ever been in youth's replies,
3470    Nor reached the ears of one like me,
An aged-old king, this one you see.
Your hands hold strength,
Your honor growing,
and your mouth
Speaks as one knowing!
If your king, that Hrethel's son,
Is slain in combat, comes undone
By sword, disease, or spear head's sting,
The Geats would but make you king,

3480 Oh keeper of these soldiers' spoil,
   No, none, I say, whose hands will toil
   Within the honor your hands bring,
   No, none but you should be their king—
   That is, if you would take the throne,
   For trust me, here I make this known
   That they would thus, this much is true,
   Yes, they would make a king of you.
   Dear Beowulf, beloved by all,
   The more I keep you in my call,
3490 The more pleased I am thus at hand
   While you stay on here in Daneland.
   Your actions have united us,
   The Danes and Geats, slaying fuss
   That once went on in warring feuds,
   Now we can claim a different mood,
   One born of friendship and affection.
   Here and now, peace is perfection,
   Sealed as long as I am king.
   My treasure hoard, my gold and rings
3500 Are given o'er to greet the men
   Who travel here, then back again
   In loving union as I stand,
   All brought by your devoted hand.
   Our ships will proffer treasures and
   Our friendship to port in your land.
   Your people live by ancient codes,
   Their hearts are trusting, lush abodes,
   Like ours, open to our friends
   Forever, love that never ends,
3510 But resolutely shut before
   Those enemies of Daneland's shore."

   A dozen more important treasures
   Hrothgar gave in loving measure,
   Seeing Beowulf delight
   In winnings from his cunning fight,
   Then orders for a safe trip back
   Came from the king, though while on track,
   Reminded Beowulf once more
   To come again to Daneland's shore.
3520 The old king kissed the hero's cheek,
   Unable to find words to speak,
   Thus grasped the shoulder of the one
   He grew to love as his own son,
   Then cried aloud, devoid of cheer,

Unable to hold back his tears.
A wise old king, the gray beard knew
His chances were a simple few
That in his life he'd ere again
See Beowulf, this noble man,
3530 Who found a place within his heart,
But still, he let hope do its part.
His love, too strong to keep within,
Burst loose as tears streamed down his chin;
His blood drew warm in longing's care.
Then Beowulf strode forth from there,
From Herot; from Hrothgar's call,
Away from that once battered hall,
And moved across the fertile lawn,
His armor shining like the dawn,
3540 Triumphant in his winning charms,
With treasures piled high in his arms.
His vessel loomed at anchor's bay;
That he could sail that very day.
And so the richness of the king
He left behind, with gold to bring
Before his lord; he traveled on
From one he had so gladly known,
That ideal king, no fault or blame
Ere lain upon that good king's name
3550 Until the seasons came and went,
And winter turned to winter, spent
The way a life will come and go,
And age no longer would bestow
The strength of youth, his stolen, gone,
Estranged and taken from his throne
The way age does time and again,
Quite stolen so from many men.


## 27

The gang of Geats, brave and young,
Marched onward with their armor hung
3560 In soldier's fashion, thus they wore
It proudly, heading to the shore.
Arriving there along the coast,
Its watcher left his daily post
Atop the hill, and whipped his horse,
Intent to take the swiftest course,
But not a warning from his mouth

Came as his steed descended south.
No, only words of grateful joy,
And said the Geats would employ
3570    The same such welcome when they got
Back home, yelled o'er his horse's trot,
A victor's yell they all would hail,
These soldiers in their shining mail.

Atop the water's taut command
Rocked back and forth upon the sand
The broad-hulled vessel loaded high
As they prepared their last goodbye.
They packed it full with every gem
And weapon's gift; of armor's brim;
3580    Of treasure, horses, rings, and gold,
As much of these as it could hold.
Against the wind, the mast up heaved,
Above the treasure they'd received—
Once Hrothgar's, now they claimed it so,
And with them, all this wealth would go.
Then Beowulf gave as reward
A golden-hilted, war-carved sword
Unto the watchman of their boat
For keeping it safe while afloat;
3590    The weapon was at best defined
An honor for one left behind.

The ship unearthed, loosed from the sand,
And thus they left behind Daneland,
Abroad the cover of the deep,
Atop the mighty ocean's keep.
The wood hull cracked and creaked to send
The Geats onward, as the wind
Pulled taut the sail and firm the rope,
As o'er the waves, the vessel's slope
3600    Trudged swiftly on across the sea
Until at last, the men could see
The ransom for their master's toil,
First seeing sights of Geat soil,
Its hills and cliffs, the wooded span,
Which warmed the hearts of every man.
Empowered by the driving force
Of wind gusts brought the ship's divorce
From open water onto land,
Exploding unto rock and sand.
3610    The harbor guards rushed forth to greet

These sailors of a single fleet,
Each guard, who had for days and days
Awaited Beowulf to praise
His men and him, beloved and brave,
Their friends who crossed the tireless waves;
They locked their ship atop the shore,
This holding statute to endure
The thriving sea while held at bay,
Not torn, unloosed and pulled away.
3620 They carried armor, ancient swords,
They brought forth jewels from the hoard,
They brought forth gold, and every gem,
They brought them with the noble whim,
That shining armor on each back,
All brought to their king, Hygelac,
Their lord and liege, giver of rings,
Their young and noble, wise-bound king
Whose hall loomed high above the sea,
The very place their king would be
3630 Surrounded by his war-hoard's kin,
Those brave and loyal Geat men.
This famous king well known for life
Lived in his hall next to his wife,
Fair Hygd, a young but wizened queen,
Well knowing far beyond her means.
The daughter of wise Hareth's womb,
This queen beat back the calling tomb
Of women's ways, like Thrith, the shrew.
Queen Hygd knew what was best to do,
3640 And gave to every Geat band
Her treasure, placed in open hands.
But Thrith, too vain, would wag her tongue,
So fierce, it was, the servants hung
Their heads and passed, for wicked tools
The princess harbored, vile and cruel,
Not her father's men, as well,
Would offer glance or look to tell
Their eyes had met with evil's lass.
No, they, as well would stoop and pass,
3650 For any but the king, himself
Who deemed to watch the wicked elf
Would sooner find a spirit loose
With their neck looped amid a noose.
Her lies, deceit, and venom sting
Would oft dilute the ruling king,
As his lieutenants signed the sheet

To pull the rug from out her feet.
Her father's loyal, trusting men
Soon found these words would not bring in
3660    The wicked Thrith, and found instead
The sheet would offer up their heads,
And through their own intentions, bade
Their lives to meet an ancient blade.
How foul a sin for such a woman
To engage in deeds uncommon
By the standards sewn by law,
To offer fear and drain the straw,
Destroying all in her attack,
Albeit one fair, or tainted black.
3670    For one whose life should be in peace,
Instead of using word's release
Intent to slay as out they spill,
Pretended, though their aim, to kill.

But Hemming's kinsmen doused her flame,
Somehow he made this woman tame.
The dwellers of his hall would tell
A different story, one known well,
Increasing swiftly through the lands,
That Thrith, now with her wedding band,
3680    Laid low her once horrific wrath,
And traveled down a different path
Once her own father cast her lot
To wed with Offa, lo, he got
That feisty daughter, this brave man.
Yes, Thrith crossed o'er the green sea's span
To join that noble soldier's side,
A fighter who would never hide,
And stood his own to never cease
Should he find war, or live in peace.

3690    They hailed her, now, as from her heart
She gave in love, she did her part
To walk in goodness, serving one,
That head of heroes, making done
Her wicked ways, torn from her head,
To treat the husband, she had wed
In admiration, as was due.
He was a man of all things true,
Both strong and brave in every worth,
As good a man as seen on earth,
3700    A spear-clad fighter without fear,

Whose gifts displayed his winning cheer.
In war, he knew not one defeat,
For he had never called retreat;
A king who ruled his kingdom well,
And kept it in his bosom's swell.
His son, brave Emer, carved a name,
This Hemming's kinsman, one the same,
This Garmund's grandson, power bound,
A gifted swordsman guarding ground,
3710    For never did this fighter yield,
Thus he became his soldiers' shield.


## 28

Then Beowulf and his whole band
Set forth along the shoreline's sand.
The earth's bold candle shone its light,
Envisioned from it's southern flight.
The journey from their harbored ship
To Hygelac made for a trip
Of briefest nature without stall
Until they reached the young king's hall,
3720    The one who slew Ongentheow,
This king and his men stood in tow,
And he would give from all he owned,
Gave treasures from his ruling throne.
The heroes walked a hastened pace
To quickly get to that loved place.
The young king knew they made it back,
This Beowulf, and all in tack,
Those brave souls who were want to roam
Had safely thus arrived back home.
3730    He sat, awaiting their decree,
Intent to greet them openly
In honor-bound exclaimed support
Once they set foot into his court.
They came, those heroes toting swords,
And Beowulf bowed to his lord,
Then stood before the Geat throne
And spoke words in a loyal tone,
King Hygelac, filled full of pride,
Brought Beowulf to sit beside
3740    His throne—this man who had survived,
And sailed triumphant, who arrived
To Geatland with gifts to bring—

He sat by kinsman and by king.
Then Hareth's daughter made the call,
Brought mead cups filled throughout the hall,
Providing ale to those brave men
Who made it to their shores again.
Unable to hold silent there,
King Hygelac confirmed with care
3750 His eagerness upon his throne
To know how all had truly gone,
That Beowulf would tell the tale
Of how, in fact, he had prevailed,
And other questions from the king
Insisted he know everything.
"Beloved and bravest Beowulf,
From hence you sailed from off this gulf,
What of your journey o'er the sea
And salty waves in war's decree
3760 To Herot, to halt the spill
Of bloodshed done in evil's will?
Were you, in all your glory's sting
Triumphant for that noble king,
Was Hrothgar's misery to end
As you endeared to help him, friend?
Yea, Grendel's brutal bloodlust burned
Within my heart, but all we learned
Inclined me to hold you at bay;
To keep you here amid my stay,
3770 Where safe, you lived, away from plight,
And left the Danes to their own fight.
Our God be praised that my eyes see
You sitting here aside from me,
As in your glory, fully armed,
You made it safe, and quite unharmed!"

Then bold Ecgtheow's brave son broke
The stirring pause; Beowulf spoke:
"My lord and king, brave Hygelac,
Of Grendel and my bold attack
3780 Upon that beast in nighttime's call
Within the borders of that hall
Abroad the scope of Daneland's shores
Are known to all; they know the score,
Where once the demon creature's face
Was seen as ruler o'er that place,
Forever eating Hrothgar's men,
And did so time and time again,

Devouring all it could see,
Providing constant misery.
3790  Then I arrived, intent to binge
My strength for those I would avenge,
And ended fast the demon's reign,
Gave punishment for all the pain
That Grendel had unleashed on them,
And now without a second whim,
I say that not a single kin
Of that foul creature born of sin,
Not even those of ancient tithes
Would ever dare to compromise,
3800  Admitting none the vicious lie,
Deceitful in their own reply,
That Grendel did in fact beat me.
I sought King Hrothgar openly,
There in his hall; where first I came,
To seek brave Healfdane's son by name,
And when he learned my reason there,
That Grendel's plight had reached my ear
And thus, I'd come to tame the beast,
He set a table for a feast,
3810  Then placed me high, that noble one,
And honored me beside his son.
His followers drank ale in toast,
Content amid their merry boast;
Then I joined in to lend my hand
In feasting with that bright-tongued band,
That wily brew, a boastful many
Loud and bold the likes as any
Bold and brass, convinced and mean,
As bold as any I have seen.
3820  His loving queen met every need,
And hurried those who bore the mead
While handing gems and rings to all
Who served her lord within his hall.
The eldest soldiers called for ale
From Hrothgar's daughter, gave a yell,
Intent that all of their demands
Were met by way of her own hand,
And Freawaru was the name
They called her, ere the young girl came.
3830  And Hrothgar plans for her to wed
With Ingeld, this Hrothgar said,
The son of noble Froda's hold.
This soldier and his daughter hold

The promise of a wedded day,
The Dane's great lord has had his say,
In hoping to deflect war's path;
Heatho-Bards whose feuding wrath
Would lay asunder many men,
A number of his Danish kin,
3840    And thus the marriage would, in common,
End the feud, done by a woman.
But he's wrong: how many wars,
How many, in our keeping score,
Have ended in a prince's bed?
A few, I say, have not met dread.
A bride can offer little peace,
Can only thwart the spear's release,
But for a while, until, too late,
The offered chance will alter fate.
3850    One day, Ingeld and all his men
Will sit there next to their brave kin,
All drinking up amid the bawl,
There drinking in that gloried hall,
Sometime once Freawaru's wed
To Ingeld, and they share a bed.
The Danes will host those ancient swords
And gleaming weapons from their hoard,
As well as armor in their keep.
Then memories kept in the deep
3860    Born of the prince's shifting mind,
Along with heroes of his kind,
As they create another measure,
Thinking of those ancient treasures,
Knowing once their fathers wore
Them all; kept them within their store,
And with those helmets, blades and shields,
Had suffered all that they could yield,
Thus loosing all in their commands,
Those swords that fell to others hands."

## 29

3870    "And seeing thus, the likes displayed,
From armor to those ancient blades,
I know Ingeld and all his men
Will feel old anger rise again.
And one of those who follow him,
A soldier bitter in his swim

Amid the ale and mead cup's might,
Will feel the heaviness of plight
And sorrow from the past reborn,
While looking on those emblems worn,
3880    And think betwixt his every breath
Of long gone war, of long gone death.
And while he sits and drinks his ale,
His harsh tongue will at length prevail,
Thus harrowing some youth's expense,
Relinquishing in dissonance
The past, embittered at its door,
Intent to start a fresh, new war:
"'Look there, my friend, o'er at that blade,
That ancient hilt; of what it's made,
3890    And then look in, I think you know
Its shape and form, who let it go.
Your father held it in his hand
The last time he could make a stand,
Your father swung it, ere he fell;
Those Danes, they slew his living well—
And slew a number of our kin—
Then stripped the bodies of those men:
Those daring Danes! One of these men,
The prince's son, perhaps, the kin
3900    Of one who brought your father down,
Dispersing treasures, swords, and crowns,
While boasting in his armor's gleam
That which, by birth, it would so seem
Should fall to you, this in your sight,
Yes, all should be claimed yours by right.'"
"Those acid words will melt the brain,
Exposing past, and death, and pain,
So suddenly, the angered youth,
In need of nothing more for proof,
3910    Will call his father's name aloud,
And slay some Dane there in the crowd—
A bloody blade made let to fall
Left in his hand will flee the hall,
His way well known through brush and wood.
But war will dawn, no premise good,
As sure as he flees on and on,
The sounds of broken oaths will dawn,
And soon the desert sun will start
To dry the love in Ingeld's heart,
3920    Thus taking from what lived inside,
And chilling him towards his bride.

I know King Hrothgar tends to think
That those he tends with gold and drink
Find love for him, Heatho-Bards,
Their lord who keeps his daughter's guard,
His Freawaru in their hearts,
This daughter sure to do her part.
But when the truth is brought to light,
The outcome will become a fight,
3930    A friendship born that cannot last
Due to the issues from the past,
The honor spoken to impress
Will be a vow made meaningless."

"But back to Grendel: I must say
Much more to you upon this day
If you, in fact, are to exact
The story I have ushered back;
My mouth must move in order to
Relay the tale, complete, to you.
3940    When heaven's gem had flown below
Unto its rest, the night in tow,
The raving monster planned and schemed
While noble men in slumber dreamed.
And thus he sought my men and I,
He sought us out that we might die,
And, lo, he came to seek death's call
Upon us there in Hrothgar's hall.
Brave Hondscio, in armor's keep,
Lay down in rest, content, asleep,
3950    And was the first from Geatland
To suffer at the demon's hand.
Alas, vile Grendel grabbed a hold
Of his still form that sleep consoled,
Then ripped and tore him limb from limb,
And gobbled up each part of him,
His fate to see a belly filled—
That noble youth the demon killed.
Yet Grendel had but just begun
His bloody tour of wicked fun,
3960    Intent to see his belly grow,
His pouch as well, stuffed full to go,
And Herot left cold and bare,
Half-empty from his rampage there.
But then he found my wishful shape,
And thought I would have no escape,
So testing his full strength in line;

His hands against these hands of mine.
The pouch that hung below his side
Was sewn of twisted dragon's hide,
3970   A large expanding bag to fill
With bodies, wrought in devil's skill;
Designed in force and forge's grasp,
In front a splendid dragon clasp
Contained the means to keep it closed,
That nothing in would be exposed.
That demon thought within his pride
He soon would place my form inside,
Then snap the clasp to firmly seal
My body in, a zesty meal.
3980   Indeed, the beast had quite a strength,
But when I stood within his length,
His strength became a useless tool,
Thus making him to be the fool."

## 30

"To tell the rest of how I slew
The demon in his frothy brew,
Paid back in full his every deed
Is not a tale thus told in speed,
Perhaps amid some poet's song,
But here and now would take too long.
3990   Just know, my king, for all my days
In Herot, your people's praise
Were sung, and will for all I know
Be hailed forever where we go.
But of that fiend, his throbbing shape
Found means to make a quick escape,
Which only gave a minute more
Unto his life, as o'er the door
Of Herot hung claw and arm,
A statement I had brought him harm.
4000   That beastly lot crept through the glen,
Endangered for his every sin,
And settled down to never wake
Beneath the bottom of his lake.
Before the sun could fully rise,
And sleepy soldiers roused their eyes,
The lord of all on Daneland's shore
Unleashed his treasures from their store,
Repaid my work in pounded gold

For beating back the creature's hold
4010    Amid the heavy hearted flame,
A battle fought in Hrothgar's name.
And as I had destroyed the beast,
He ushered in a heavy feast;
The hall grew full of songs and ale,
And others simply told their tales.
One aging Dane spoke in a rhyme
Of paste events and long gone times,
As Hrothgar would, from time to time,
Evoke the melody of chime
4020    While strumming on the silver strings
Abroad his harp to make it sing,
Thus telling tales of wonderment,
A brave king singing his lament
O'er good and evil in their truth—
And other times the laden proof
Of growing old, remembering
When he still held a soldier's sting
Amid his strength, the glory won.
Then he would weep when he was done,
4030    That old and wizened ruler, wise
By all that passed before his eyes,
As many winters he had ruled,
A man not easily thus fooled,
Remembering the things he knew,
That ancient past, a time now through.

And so we ate and drank in joy.
When darkness, then, in its employ
Thus fell upon the feasting lot,
4040    As evil, soon, the hall forgot,
But in the shadows, undercover,
Came a beast, lo, Grendel's mother
Lurked below in heavy breath,
Come to avenge her offspring's death,
Intent to usher hate and pain
Inflicted on that house of Danes.
She found success, that demon spawn,
And broke before the coming dawn
By reaching in those golden walls
4050    Amid that glory-ridden hall
And slew Aeschere, someone who
Had long been loyal, fierce and true
To Hrothgar's reign, until his end,
An elder warrior; a friend.

But when the sun burst into sight,
There would not be a loud pyre's light,
For not a log would reap a flame,
Nor would there be the ashes' claim
Of bringing dust from fleshy wake:
4060    The demon's claw made no mistake
And took from there his lifeless shape,
Returning to her dismal drape
Beneath the water's churning sway.
Then Hrothgar wept the length of day,
For though his eyes had cried before
O'er many men, this time the score
Cut deeper, hurting him far worse,
Polluted by that demon's curse.
He pleaded in your name to me,
4070    Half tearful as his choked decree
Relinquished off his open lips,
Inquiring that I make the trip,
To seek an honor higher, still,
Below that murky water's fill,
Expressing all my eyes would see,
The treasures he would give to me.

Unable to do naught but right,
I dove below and sought the fight,
I sought that witch, corrupt and wild,
4080    Quite angered hence I slew her child,
And, lo, we fought, her claw, my hand,
Engrossed in one another's stand
Until the murky water cast
The color red from blood; at last
I groped the answer to my call,
As there upon that ancient wall
Beneath the depths, a mighty sword
Became the means hung in accord
To seek fulfillment's even thread,
4090    And lo, I severed off her head.

I barely made it out alive,
But death was not allowed to thrive.
And thus the Dane's great lord endeared
To fill my heart when I appeared,
And offered his wealth openly,
Great gems and gold rewarded me."

## 31

"He lived his days as good kings must:
I gathered all things in his trust,
No treasure given for my might
4100    In victory left from my sight.
He opened up his treasure hoard
And let me choose what I adored,
From gems and bracelets, armor, swords,
This all for me on your accord,
My king, so done to be your friend,
And show my love that does not end.
To own your favor holds me still,
For I can naught but do your will:
My family is all but gone,
4110    Save you, my king upon your throne,
Yes, all but you, brave Hygelac,
Are gone, and thus I have come back,
Success in what I had to do,
My life and sword I offer you."

Then Beowulf altered his manner,
Sending for the boar head banner,
Helmet, silver armor, and
That shining sword with golden bands:
"This war-wear was Hrothgar's reward,
4120    The helmet, armor, and this sword,
My treasure from his wise, old grip.
Upon returning from my trip,
He longed for me to tell the tale
From whom and whence these treasures hailed.
His older brother, Hergar, owned
These gifts until he left the throne
In death to Hrothgar: though his son
Had proven worthy, what was done
Was done, and thus for brave Herward,
4130    The throne was not his just reward.
And now, I give these gifts to you,
A sign of trust between us two:
Their past is one for kings to tell,
So may they ever serve you well!"

And after all of this was said,
Four horses by their reigns were led
Into the room, compelled to neigh,
Alike, they were, in every way.

Hence, Beowulf brought for his king
4140  A hoard of gifts from gold to rings,
Some horses, too, to seal his trust—
The sort of thing a leader must,
Not seeking harm for those he trained,
No harmful deeds to be explained,
Nor death sought in the darkest pit,
For his men knew he was legit.
King Hygelac held faith in him,
His nephew, leaning on his whim
In times of war for strength's employ,
4150  There resting on each other's joy.
Then Beowulf gave up the gem
Sweet Wealhtheow had given him,
That necklace in its shining state
He passed to Hygd, love to relate,
And lo, the king's wife marveled on
As from atop her ruling throne,
The hero gave in noble courses
Three divine exclusive horses;
Taking them at his behest,
4160  Then wore the necklace o'er her breast.

So bold Ecgtheow's son aligned
Himself in honor's gloried shrine,
And proved himself as no one could,
Fulfilling all by what was good:
Not slaying friends in drunken rage,
His heart prepared with growing age,
Not savage in its beating mark,
For God dwelled there, defeating dark,
And Beowulf conceived to sift
4170  Through peril, holding to the gift
The Father of all men at length
Had given him, his precious strength,
Used only in those times of war,
And when his might bade its outpour,
His efforts were of noble gain,
So bravely done without refrain.
And yet when youth his frame adorned,
He often found his presence scorned;
The Geats thought he was a waste
4180  And wrote him off in utter haste.
When ere he sat within their hall,
And men came at their ruler's call,
Made rich by him, paid for their skill,

He held none of the king's good will.
They thought the lad was lazy, slow,
And weak, but noble in his show.
But now the tide had turned on them,
And none claimed glory quite like him,
As any insult from the past
4190 Was taken back, and did not last,
For Beowulf held wonder's fame,
And his alone was glory's name.

Then Hygelac, that noble king,
Called forth in wonderment to bring
His father's great and mighty blade,
Its golden gleam brought and displayed,
Its working none could better boast,
This ancient sword had meant the most
To Beowulf's grandfather's care,
4200 And now it loomed before him there.
The king then placed its golden clap
On Beowulf's unknowing lap,
And gave him seven thousand hides
Of land, a sharing gift of pride,
Complete with houses, ground, and all.
In Geatland, the open call
Held room for king and prince alike;
Their fathers built with long gone pikes
The fences, buildings, and the fields—
4210 King Hygelac kept greater yields,
For he was high upon the throne
And all thus followed him alone.

When time had passed its woven thread,
And Hygelac at last was dead,
And Heardred, his noble son,
Who ruled in place had come undone—
Met with an end in battle's call
Against the Swedes, who bade him fall
By bashing in his shield, for then
4220 The Swedes had passed his gallant men
And ushered forth the king's demise
Amid their stolen battle cries.
Yes, then, when Hygd's one son was gone,
Did Beowulf ascend the throne,
And ruled the Geats long and well,
A king like none before could tell.

## 32

When fifty winters turned the page,
And Beowulf grew ripe with age,
A dragon woke from slumber's keep,
4230    Aroused amid its ancient sleep
From darkened dreams composed of evil,
Bringing terror to his people.
In a tower made of stone,
The beast had slept for years, unknown,
Devoid of spewing forth the wrath
It held beneath the secret path;
A man discovered by mistake
The entrance to the sleeping drake,
And sneaking in a quiet measure,
4240    Stumbled o'er an ancient treasure.
Pagan gems and ruby stones,
As well as gold and rotting bones
The dragon guarded, slumbering,
Until some hands went fumbling
In greedy manner, dazed in awe
By all the man within there saw.
And groping without looking up,
He stole a jewel-crested cup,
Then motioned while his heartbeat sped,
4250    As from that place he amply fled.
But now the dragon did not hide,
Not theft or self, and soon was spied;
It pulsed and thrived in darkened skies
As Geatland soon heard its cries,
The sound emitting sudden danger,
Knowing well its wicked anger.


## 33

But the man had not arrived
To steal or loot; though stealing thrived
And woke the dragon deep within,
4260    Arousing hatred's beastly sin.
The saddened truth, the thief, indeed,
Came not for theft, but more from need.
He was a slave mistreated by
His masters, beaten foot to eye,
And ran away from man's disgrace,

But had nowhere, no hiding place;
That's when he found the secret trail,
And used it to his own avail.
And once within, his fear released,
4270    For there he saw the sleeping beast
Which yawned and motioned just a bit.
Not wanting to dare waken it,
In fear and awe, he turned to leave
In hope his life would yet receive
Another day to anti up,
While pilfering the jeweled cup.

That tower was completely full
Of ancient riches' gleaming lull,
Relinquished their long years before
4280    By way of one left to endure
As only one, the last within
His noble race, no other kin,
That olden hoard of gems and gold
Configured in its darkest hold
A final mark abruptly penned,
A dynasty that reached its end.
When death had stolen every slate,
The soldier left to mourn their fate
Expected soon the very same,
4290    To be the next one death would claim,
Regarding truth within him told,
The thought of all those gems and gold
He guarded o'er those many years
Could not hold back the jaunting fears,
And though he knew his stock was stronger,
Those gems could not please much longer.
Crested cups of golden jewels,
Armor wrought by flaming tools,
The relics, gems, and ancient weapons,
4300    Brought beneath the stone protection
In that tower by the sea,
Below the crag, a walled decree,
A citadel in bolted locks,
No windows, only waves and rocks
Before, behind there on the shore;
It did not even have a door.
And when the silent moment broke,
Within the tower, one man spoke:
"These treasures here, in noble worth,
4310    I give them to you, mother earth,

For none are left alive to see
These riches guarded once by me.
When time began, these gems and gold
Were yours, oh, earth, kept in your fold;
Allow them thus another turn
As to you they must now return.
My people have been washed away
By war and horror day by day,
Their eyes no longer seeing light,
4320    Nor any of your lush delights,
As now the door of life has closed,
And happiness has been disposed.
No one remains to hold a cup,
Or lift a mighty war-blade up.
Nobody leads, nor can one follow,
Thus I sit alone in sorrow.
Hammered golden helmets sitting
Crack and waste, no end befitting
Such as those delightful tops
4330    Which once brought weapons to a stop,
For not a hand remains to shine
Or polish them to their refine,
As all arrived in death together,
Hands immoveable forever.
What of metal mail gear worn
In battles, those that once adorned
The bodies of these fallen men,
As swords bit hard atop their spin
And blades crashed down into the shields,
4340    Thus driving on the fighters' yields?
They will all rust to fade and dim
The same as those once owning them.
These treasures will not leave to seek
The shores of other stony peaks,
No gems abroad, nor gleaming swords
Will follow long behind their lords.
The harp's melodious reply,
The soaring hawk up in the sky
Upon its wings before the hall,
4350    The stallion heeding someone's call
Within its neighing, whining guard
While tramping o'er the lush courtyard—
All gone, each beast and bird born brave,
Their masters hurtled to the grave!"

Thus sad in heart, the soldier said
His grieved lament for those long dead,
And walked the earth a joyless soul
Until the time death took control,
Forsaking him to be the last,
4360    An emblem of forgotten past.

A savage stalker of the night,
One uttering in fiery spite,
A dragon spewing flame by tongue,
Discovered something ere it hung
Its scaly neck below to see
The treasure waiting openly.

The beast men fear within the cloak
Of darkness came in ashy smoke,
A lighted fire seeking caves
4370    And ancient ruins yet to stave,
But when it sought the tower's hold,
It came upon those heaps of gold.
And then it made itself a home
From which it deemed it would not roam,
Upon the stones and silver hues
It would not leave, nor could not use.

So mankind's foe, exceeding might,
Slept long within its dreary night
Amid those walls of olden stone,
4380    Atop its gleaming, beaming throne.
Three hundred winters hence amassed,
As for the beast, time slowly passed
Until an absence woke it up.
A thieving hand removed a cup,
Desiring naught but to appease
His master, begging on his knees
Forgiveness, sought and bought in sight
Of such a cup, which brought delight
To such a needy lord, indeed,
4390    Who clutched its ancient form with greed,
Amazed by runes and carvings strewn
Abroad the likes he had not known.
Thus peace begotten for the slave
Came from the cup; new life it gave
Amid his master's altered stage,
But roused the dragon's ardent rage.

It turned, and burned in fevered wrath,
While sniffing for the robber's path,
And when his tracks were back in bounds,
4400    The scent at last the dragon found,
Unleashing from beyond its throne
The place the thief had come and gone.

That man survived the course he chose,
Had nearly touched the dragon's nose
And scaly head, and yet alive
He found himself as jaws in size
The likes no man had seen in years
Aroused to snap and chew as sheers,
But God is good and gave a pair
4410    Of silent feet to speed him there
As far from in the tower's keep
As he could go without a peep.

The dragon traced the robber's moves
Along those trodden, stony grooves,
Intent to find the thieving creep
Who robbed its silver and its sleep;
It circled round and round again,
But could not find that tiny man,
Determined to engulf his shape
4420    Within its flame, or snatch his nape,
But past the tower fled the man,
A silent target as he ran,
And in the woods where he had gone,
His presence was no longer known.

The beast stormed back atop its hoard,
Amassing vengeful, hateful chords
Of discontent; a fiery flood,
And wanted nothing less than blood.
It planned revenge within its hole,
4430    Accounting for the thing he stole,
That cup the thief had ushered on,
That item missing from its throne.
Then perching o'er those ancient stones,
It counted eagerly alone
The passing of the hourglass,
Awaiting day to slowly pass,
Until the candle wrought by He
Who ruled the earth eternally
At length extinguished unto dark.

4440 And lo, its flame began to spark
Until the dragon's feral rage
Could be unleashed from in its cage,
Devouring the realm in flame,
A vengeance none could dare to tame,
As wings contorted, bringing death
Wrought by the dragon's flaming breath.
And when the sun had gone from sight
Revealing finally the night,
Corruption offered nothing sad,
4450 For lo, the dragon's heart was glad:
Illuminated in its ire,
How it had longed to sear with fire
The whole, its enemies at hand,
Impatient for this one command.
The people suffered fearfully,
As none were spared the beast's decree,
But when their danger reached the ears
Of Beowulf, their fitful tears,
The fate awaiting him was worse
4460 Beneath the dragon's raging curse,
As underneath the creature's flame
The hero's trouble swiftly came.


## 34

Volcanic vengeance spewed in blaze
And smoky sulfur crafting haze,
The while the dragon torched each house
Within its flaming, blazing douse.
They peered in terror as the fire
Rose in retribution's pyre:
For, lo, the angered dragon meant
4470 To slay them all in its intent.

And in the darkened state of night,
For miles was seen the dragon's spite,
As embers like the sun at dawn
Broke through the dark and made it known,
Long miles revealing burning land,
The hateful tokens of its brand
And brutal malice, spreading like
A warning o'er the burning pike
To all the flames would soon ingest,
4480 Those Geats who disturbed its rest.

And when it stopped the flaming shower,
It retreated to its tower,
To the riches hoard o'er,
Before the sunshine lit the shore.
Enfolding Geatland in flame,
Beneath old stones, the dragon came
To rest again upon its throne;
It trusted in those olden stones,
The barricade that stood erect,
4490    And thought the walls would thus protect.

But trusting stone would prove far wrong.
The peoples' cries did not take long
To reach the ear and pierce in sting,
Arousing Beowulf, the king,
Announcing that his hall, his throne,
And many buildings now were gone,
Dissolved beneath the dragon's breath,
As Geats crackled, burned to death.
Their words wrought wretchedness within,
4500    As sorrow clipped the thought of sin
And Beowulf looked to his heart
For reasons they had come apart.
He cursed himself by what they saw,
Assuming one of God's own laws
Had broken under his command,
And thus, throughout the burning land,
The anger of the Father's flare
Was given to his people there.
His breast grew full of sorrow's bind,
4510    And darkness crept into his mind,
Thus Beowulf bore on his face
A deepened frown, a dismal place
Where once had been a joyful stance
Now seemed a lonely circumstance.
But now the hall that once belonged
Before the shore and had been wronged
By searing heat in molten flame
Which beat across its sturdy frame
Erupting from the dragon's source,
4520    Aligned, designed until the course
Before the fire's burning tone
Devoured it till it was gone.
The Geats suffered in the singe
Of dragon flame, and thus revenge

Began to weave a web within
The heart of Beowulf's chagrin.

Preparing for the battlefield,
He called for such a battle-shield
Thus wielded, wrought and shaped in fashion
4530     From the ore of iron ration,
Knowing wood would be a waste
When covered with emblazoned baste
Depicted as flamboyant beams
Of flaming, scorching blazing streams,
Nor linden in its wooden fold
Would serve beneath the dragon's scold,
Unnerving him unto his death
When greeting fleeting dragon's breath.

And thus his days on earth would end,
4540     That noble prince would soon defend
Himself his last, and life would cease,
But he would not give up in ease,
No, he would take the dragon's days
From it as well, remove its stay
Atop its gleaming, beaming throng,
The loot it guarded for so long.

Alone, the king would heed the fight,
A testament to all his might,
Avoiding leading other men
4550     Against an odd they could not win.
He saw no fear, or even thought
On claws and wings, or jaws thus sought—
He fought the likes of them before,
In odds much worse, a secret war,
And won the day, surviving all
By bringing demons to a crawl
And then to death in Herot,
The home of one no one forgot,
The king, Hrothgar's haunted hall
4560     Where Grendel came to maim and bawl.
He slew the demon and his mother,
Tearing them from one another.
Then he fought in battle's store,
And then came Hygelac's bold war
To halt the Frisian's marching dance,
Beside his lord till circumstance
Crept in, and lo, the high king sank

As from his side, a deep cut drank
The life from him, and yea, he fell,
4570   No more among his men to dwell,
For in the heat of conflict's horde,
He fell beneath a rushing sword,
The Geat's lord and marveled king
Gone down to earth amid death's sting.
Then Beowulf escaped the wrath
Brought by the Frisian's warring path
And swam along to freedom's shore
While taking armor in his store.
In fact he totaled thirty sets,
4580   Removed from those with no regrets,
Those thieving Franks, who robbed the dead
As their shapes moved the river's thread.
His sword was all he came to give,
Deciding thus they must not live,
And Beowulf slew in his swim,
Until they gladly ran from him
In shameful spite, those few alive,
Who reached their shore intent to thrive.

So Beowulf returned his hand
4590   In sadness, reaching Geatland,
It seemed one of the only few
To make it back and thus renew
Morale among his people's ranks,
But came so to remorseful banks.
When he arrived amidst the frowns,
The queen, brave Hygd, offered the crown,
For her own son, bold Heardred,
She trusted not with foreign tread,
Unsure her son could thus defend
4600   Their kingdom from those war would send.
But Beowulf refused the crown,
And quickly, swiftly turned her down,
Responding in a noble mirth
That while the one her womb gave birth
Was still alive, his lord's own son,
His life was his, and thus as one
The Geats gave support that spread
To their new king, brave Heardred.
Thus Beowulf lent all his might
4610   To Heardred, the king by right,
Fulfilling duty to his lord,
By way of word; by way of sword,

A loving heart to guide and see
What Heardred lacked openly.
Endeavors of the warmest sort,
Along with love's engrossed support,
The king received within good will,
As Beowulf passed on his skill.

Othere's sons began to file
4620    Across the shore in their exile,
The Swedish troupe hoped for direction,
Shielded in the king's protection,
Setting foot on Geat soil,
There breaking from Onela's toil.
This King Onela, son-in-law
To Healfdane's son, marched on in awe,
For he became a gloried king.
Deliverer of golden rings;
He brought an army, battle-bred,
4630    To Geatland, amassing dread.
King Heardred supplied support
To those he promised from the port
Of Sweden's lands, and thus he gave
His life, and not a soul could save
His form from what Onela brought,
That Swedish king had only sought
One thing, the death of Heardred
For aiding those of whom had fled
His ruling thumb, and nothing more.
4640    When this was done, he left those shores,
Returning to his Swedish throne,
Thus leaving Geatland alone,
And when he left, the open pool
Of empty kingship left the rule
Up to the next of kin in line,
Thus Beowulf held by design
The throne of Geatland, and well
He ruled them in his joyous swell!

## 35

But Beowulf did not forget
4650    The way in which he felt regret
O'er losing his companion's son,
The king, brave Heardred, undone
By warring hands of angry Swedes.

As soon as he had met the needs
Of those remaining rebels there
Upon his shore; within his care
By lending fighters, gold, and might
To Eadgils, a wretched slight
Unto the Swedes, Othere's son,
4660    Across the seas, a battle won
Assured revenge in every tone,
And gave to him the Swedish throne,
A bitter conflict won in pain,
As king Onela thus was slain.

So Ecgtheow's bold son survived;
His legend prospered ere it thrived,
No matter what the dangers were,
The battles fought a brew; a stir,
Forever one to triumph o'er
4670    What lay his way; what held in store
In honor and bravado's keep,
Until that day a fated sweep
With pulsing, flaming dragon's breath
Conceived his end, and brought him death.

A dozen angered men arose
Beside their king's embittered pose
And walked until the lair thus loomed,
Where lived the creature who had doomed
The countryside by warring flame,
4680    Thus to its home, the marchers came;
And Beowulf already knew
The feat that stirred that monster's brew,
Enraging it to open fire,
Burning in its hot desire.
Lo, that cup had passed to him,
Had traveled o'er from limb to limb,
And gone from slave to master's care,
And then to he who led them there,
And fate had turned its page again.
4690    For in the front, that very man,
The thieving slave who brought the lot
Of dragon's scorching, flaming hot
Corruptive essence on them all,
And caused the burning of that hall
Which guarded once the rushing shore,
To him, the Geats passed this chore,
And so he went before them then,

Afraid of both the beast and men,
And took them ere his feet would roam
4700 Until they reached the dragon's home.
He brought them to those olden stones,
Locked in the earth's unchanging tones,
Where ocean waves imbued their stock
Erupting o'er the jutting rocks,
A scene to him that was obscene,
As he became the last, thirteen,
A number not of luck's device;
The thief's dismay cut like a knife.

Then Beowulf stopped in his stride
4710 To hear of what was heaped inside;
The treasures in that ancient hold,
The piles of gems and heaps of gold.
Distressed and wakeful in its whim,
The dragon lurked, awaiting him.
No man would get that armor cheap,
That golden gear and brimming heap!

The battle-laden king's repose
Upon the shore where others chose
To wish him well was worn and brief.
4720 His heart was weighty, full of grief,
And Beowulf, under control,
Alerted in his deepest soul
A sense and stature wearing late,
Detecting pieces of his fate,
But not in fear, nor feudal rage,
Just knowledge coming from his age.
His armor, strong in its design,
No longer shaped the outer line
Of what had once been seen as harm,
4730 Now just a hanging, drooping arm,
And like his arm, now hung his heart.
He knew his soul might soon depart
From in his body's aging shape,
And death surround him like a cape;
His blood might leak from in its mesh,
And life would end from in his flesh.

His courage took a final stroke,
And there before his men, he spoke:
"My younger years were carved in war,
4740 But I survived them, shore to shore;

The smell of battle's bloody sting,
I still remember everything.
When seven winters came and went,
Old Hrethel summoned in consent
For me to leave my father's fold,
And thus he filled my lap with gold,
That gracious king instructed me,
Just glad I sat atop his knee.
He never favored any more
4750   His children, nor did he adore
Them less, for mine was one the same
With any of his princes' names—
The eldest, Herebeald, then
Came Haethcyn, next of my lord's kin,
And last, my king, brave Hygelac,
Those were the sons in Hrethel's pack.
When Herebeald met with an end,
It tore a rift that could not mend,
A hunting trip gone far awry,
4760   That horrid way he came to die.
His brother, Haethcyn, shot his bow
And launched an arrow in its flow,
But when the tip struck fleshy hide,
It missed the mark and lunged inside
The heart of Herebeald instead,
And left that son of Hrethel dead.
The guilty one did not deny
The horrid crime, nor question why
When all came down beneath his breath,
4770   No vengeance could refund that death,
No punishment could seek the right,
No, none at all within their sight.
So with the elder man whose son
Engages sin in matters done
Against the king, the end result
Will be the gallows' hanging cult:
The father's watchful, teary gaze
Corrupts his heart in deep malaise,
As he can naught but stand and stare
4780   The while his son is hanging there
Upon the gallows' fatal noose,
Convinced death was not his to choose,
Expressing grief, a hapless fool,
There seeing flesh become a tool
So used to feed the raven's peck,
His body hanging by its neck.

The graybeard elder wants to cry,
To pluck revenge, an eye for eye,
But cannot, so he stares again
4790    At what had once been called a man.
And every time the sunlight beams,
He lives the moment while he screams,
Remembering his son who died,
A mournful man bereft inside.
No other son would ere replace
The image of his dead one's face.
No heir in line, no future bright
Exuded from a father's spite,
For one who lived to see such death,
4800    Exuding sorrow in each breath.
The world where his first son had dwelled
Became a wasted, world, compelled
By nothing cheerful in its state,
Extinguished by his son's poor fate;
The father who has lost his son
Has seen it all, has come undone.
So soldiers sleep among the dead
In open coffins, or a bed,
Devoid of reason in their keep
4810    Yet either way it is they sleep;
No pleasure left in anything,
The harp is hushed, thus does not sing,
And all once fresh has spoiled, rotten,
Hope and faith have been forgotten."


# 36

"Crying, he crawls to his bed:
The earth, his home, both full of dread.
And so it was in Hrethel's sight,
When Herebeald joined the night
Which none shall rise to see new light,
4820    Unending torment sealed in spite.
His sorrow came without relief,
And in his heart lived only grief.
The killer walked; no love for him
Was found inside the father's whim,
And never would again, it seemed,
But not a thing in life, nor dreamed
Could aid his hurt, no word-filled horde,
Nor battle-heavy bloody sword,

Not war in passions born in hate,
4830 Not feud or combat left to fate,
Not anything, it seemed, could awe,
For nothing mattered, even law.
The ache within held no relief,
His heart could only live in grief,
Or leave itself, no more to live,
The only choices it could give.
However, he found hope in spite,
And ere he died, he sought God's light.

When death arose and struck him down,
4840 Then Haethcyn came to wear the crown,
And Hygelac won riches, too,
Divided up amongst those two.
And then the war of bloody deeds
Engaged the Geats and the Swedes,
Across the waters, battle-brew
Engulfed the minds of all who knew
The mighty Hrethel slept below.
And thus they came, a war in tow,
The sons of Ongentheow's mirth
4850 Assumed their plans could weather birth
Without the pains of failed disguise,
And openly before the eyes
Of all in Geatland attacked,
Pretending nothing but ransacked,
And raided, pillaging the land,
Unyielding, thirsty, greedy hands,
And near Hreosnaburg's accord,
A many Geat met the sword
Of thieving Swedish men's delight.
4860 But lo, my people took the fight,
Repaying death for death, indeed,
And battled hard against the Swedes,
Though one who sought that sweet revenge,
The brother who had wrought the cringe
Upon his father's aching heart—
The very one who did his part—
The king, that Haethcyn who had reigned
The Geats in his title gained
By way of death now likewise, dead,
4870 Rewarded by the cunning thread
Which wove itself into my lord,
His end came from a Swedish sword.
But when the light of dawn arrived,

Late Beowulf

His slayer's veins, which pulsed and thrived,
No longer pumped their bloody flow,
And Hygelac's companion's blows
Defeated in avenging shade
The Swedish men upon each blade.
When Ongentheow sought his foe,
4880    Brave Eofor returned his woe
By lashing out until a crack
Upon his helmet knocked him back,
Proceeding to endear its lull
Until at last it cleaved his skull.
And lo, it forced the Swede's king down,
A bitter, bleeding futile frown
Across his lips as to the ground,
His body slumped, the only sound
Remaining in the sight displayed
4890    Arrived by Eofor's own blade
Assimilating victory,
Depriving Ongentheow's plea
For life, as through his dying choke.
His ending came in one swift stroke,
The while the soldier slaying him
Exuded triumph from his brim.
The treasures Hygelac gave me,
The land, the gold, his firm decree,
The riches, all at length, I paid
4900    By lending him my battle-blade,
Begotten by my able hand
As was allowed by Fate's demand.
He never had the slightest need
For Dane, or Goth, nor even Swede,
No man abroad amid his fold,
No mercenary paid with gold,
Imbibed by wealth to stay astride
And fight along my liege's side.
My blade could boast a mighty swell,
4910    A better symbol bringing Hell
To those whose lives it wished to drink,
As down below, their souls would sink.
Alone, I strode to go before
The many foes in every war,
And so it shall forever be,
As long as here my blade serves me
Today as it has in the past,
And will tomorrow, ere it lasts.
I slew Daghrefin, Huga's champ,

4920    A mighty hero from their camp,
       The mighty fiend who took the life
       Of Hygelac with his long knife,
       Then looted from his lifeless corpse:
       My hands retrieved without remorse
       That necklace clasped behind the nape
       Of Hygd, once Wealhtheow's own drape,
       And so it never reached the hands
       Of Daghrefin's chief in command.
       He died in battle, ere we fought,
4930    That battle-banner prince who sought
       A glory taken in his might,
       But could not beat my strong hold's bite.
       My sword in hand did not befell
       The man I fought, no, I must tell
       The way I used naught but my grip
       To take his breath and see him slip
       Into the grip of death's confine.
       I bore him in these arms of mine
       And pressed him inward to my chest,
4940    To prove indeed I was the best.
       And so his body cracked and curved,
       A crushing end, one he deserved,
       And so I broke his bones into,
       And watched the blood from out him spew
       When ere I reached within the part
       I tore and ripped from it his heart.
       And now, again within this measure,
       I shall battle for this treasure,
       Forcing on that demon's horde
4950    My hands as well as with my sword."

       And there before the crushing coast
       The words that carved the final boast
       From Beowulf were uttered hard
       Before those who were keeping guard:
       "I say to all before me here
       I never knew the taste of fear;
       My youth met countless battlefields.
       Now old, I say I will not yield,
       Still seeking fame and glory, still,
4960    Intent to make the final kill,
       If now the dragon, yet this hour,
       Will unwind from in its tower,
       Daring thus to face my sword,
       Relinquishing its bounty-horde."

And then he made his final vow
By each companions' drooping brow,
His last amount of speaking done
Before the ears of everyone:
"No sword or weapon I would use
4970    If simple hands could crush or bruise
The dragon, slain the very same
As one, yea, Grendel was his name,
That fiend who lost his battle-whim,
My hands would tear it limb from limb.
But flaming breath will burst among
My body, and its poison tongue
Will hiss and rasp its biting stance.
I feel no shame, the circumstance
Is one that needs a sword and shield,
4980    Bold armor worn upon the field,
Thus guarding me against the beast
Who comes upon my flesh to feast:
I will not flee, nor will it tame
My moral with its beating flame,
I plan to stand till fate aligns
And offers up the last design
Consigned upon the final spin,
Deciding which of us shall win.
The battle honor is my balm,
4990    My heart is solid, firmly calm.
To further boast would be absurd;
I do not need a boastful word.
Atop this hill, wait for me, men.
Protect our war-gear, and your skin.
We soon will see who will survive
This gruesome conflict, leave alive,
Still standing when the fight is done,
Victorious; the battle won.
No other choice have I today
5000    But to go forth, intent to slay
This beast, for none but I can stand
Against this evil thing's command.
I would not let another try,
Not even if this means goodbye.
And of the treasure, in its hold,
The dragon's gems and all the gold
It guards within this tower's keep
Will come to me, or war will sweep

Away my soul in flaming breath,
5010    Consuming me unto my death!"

Then Beowulf, still bold and strong,
Arose to take the dragon's throng,
His shield arresting by his side,
His chain mail rustling in each stride
Upon his breast and body's beat,
As calmly he moved on his feet
In confidence toward the place
Beneath the cliffs he would embrace:
No coward would have posed the dare
5020    To ever let his feet fall there!

And then the bravest battle king
Who stole from fighters everything,
The man who fought a dozen wars,
Had weathered swords and battle sores,
Beheld the stony archway's feat
And felt the baring, beating heat
Exuding from the dragon's breath,
The emblem of a certain death,
Deluging down the corridor,
5030    Escaping through the secret door,
A scorching blaze too hot for those
Who stood behind their hero's pose,
A streaming, steaming smoky blast
To bar the man from walking past.

And so the Geat king avowed
To call the beast, as in a loud
And fervent tone in anger's mirth,
He bade it loosen from its girth
5040    And made his sword drop to his side
While in the cavern's hold, he cried
And coaxed the beast within the rock
To come and greet his steady stock,
And lo, the words rung deep and clear
And hung within the dragon's ear.

The beast arose, an angry lot
To seek the man, its temper hot,
And nothing short of battle's brew
Would follow for these ardent two.
5050    A steaming haze erupted first,
Configured in a blazing burst

Which passed through stone around each nook,
And then the land around them shook.

His iron shield swung in its place
And Beowulf stood to embrace
The flames erupting through the hold,
As he held ever firm and bold.

The dragon wound and then unwound
From off its heap, the thumping sound
5060    Of heated passion in its heart
Compelling it to thus depart
And reap the battle waiting for
Its presence to
Burst through the door.
The ancient sword of Beowulf,
Unsheathed and shining on the gulf,
Awaited combat's bloody shade,
Those razor edges of his blade.
The dragon came to claim its bet,
5070    And both grew ready, poised and set
On nothing short of murder's deed,
Intent to see the other bleed.
The Geat prince held fast and firm,
And lo, the beast brought not a squirm,
So waited he behind the round
Constructed shield, to hold his ground,
His armor gleaming, calling fate
The while the war-king stood to wait.
The dragon lunged in torrid might,
5080    Expulsing fire in its flight
Along with smoky gray-clad haze,
Prepared to reach the end of days.

Volcanic pressure doused the shield,
And for a time, it did not yield,
As sure as Beowulf had felt,
But soon the heat caused it to melt,
And on that day passed for the first
A time when all fell for the worst
As lo, that famous warlord's state
5090    Had naught for glory, naught for fate
As fate, indeed, had gone awry
And left the Geat there to die.
This held no secret in his heart,
But Beowulf would do his part,

Avenging deaths, exposing pride,
And so he struck the dragon's hide.
Admittance granted there beneath
Exposed the beast for but a brief
And fading glimpse amid the smoke,
5100    As through the skin, it seemed he broke
For blood erupted, but in vain,
Not deep enough in its domain
Internally to bring much harm,
Though oozing liquid, thick and warm,
Cascaded from the contact's stroke,
That ancient blade, alas, it broke.

The dragon grew enraged in pain,
Unleashing in a spewing strain
Destruction from the north to south
5110    As flames went forth from its hot mouth.
Astride the conflict while assailed,
The Geat king knew he had failed,
For boasting fled the closing door,
And battles won, the victor's war,
Attempted not a single chance
To cross his mind, his circumstance
Was not to be a winning story,
Passing from his lips the glory.
Steel that once had long prevailed
5120    For Beowulf that moment failed,
That ancient sword so finely wrought
Deserted him and left him caught
Amid the net that fate would weave,
And from the earth he soon would leave.
Beneath the raging dragon's breath,
Belittled, Beowulf sensed death,
Unwilling to lie down and die
Without one last avenging try
Before the darkness covered space,
5130    And took him to another place,
A journey all alive endure
As death accepts the brief allure
Of what short time a human's birth
Leads into dying while on earth.

Revolving in its hastened flight,
The dragon dove, enraged in spite,
Encouraged by the sight it saw
As Beowulf dropped back in awe

Of overwhelming flames and heat,
5140 Which joined to knock him off his feet.
The dragon's blazing blasts surged in,
And Beowulf felt cloth and skin
Enraptured in the searing flame
From one the hero could not tame,
And all around the rising tide
Of flames licked in from every side—
The mighty king amid the smolder
Now became a fallen soldier.
No one came to lend him aide,
5150 No friend to help the king who stayed
Alone, his bold and trusted men
Returning to the forest glen,
Escaping, fleeing for their good,
Despondent, running in the wood.
But one remained, stood firm and fast,
Remembering his leader's past,
And as a man of honor must,
He thought of kinship and of trust.

# 37

The name of he who did not run
5160 Was Wiglaf, son of Weohstan,
A daring soldier when in fight;
His family had taken flight
From Sweden, but his heart and sword
Were Beowulf's, whom he adored.
His eyes beheld his most loved king,
And saw the warlord's suffering.
Remembering the many things
His gracious kin and noble king
Bestowed upon his family,
5170 The weapons, chain mail by decree,
The golden heirlooms, gems and stones,
All gifts begotten from the throne
Of Beowulf, the greatest king,
Bequeathed before the Waegmundings,
Those vast estates, each silver cup,
Thus Wiglaf bade his mind made up.
He heaved his shield above his head,
Unleashed his sword from out its bed—
An olden heirloom, once the blade
5180 Of Eanmund, a corpse displayed

By Weohstan who slew the man
When fleeing Sweden's current plan,
And courting safety, found instead
His death when seeking Heardred.
So Wiglaf's father came to see
The king, presenting openly
Those items once his nephew's own,
Exposed them there before the throne,
Those weapons of a man, defiant,
5190   Chain mail linked, and sword some giant
Crafted in its long cooled flame,
Another time from which it came,
As well, the helmet made of gold,
All kept within Weohstan's hold.
The king had given all of these
To Eanmund before degrees
Of feuding swept their love away,
And hatred took its place to stay.
When Weohstan had carried in
5200   The items of the king's dead kin,
No word was offered other than
The order for the winning man
To take the armor, sword and all
For coming to Onela's call.
So Weohstan amassed in cheer
The items claimed, and through the years
Awaited such a time and place
When Wiglaf would find their embrace
As noble and as firm as him,
5210   And earn much honor wearing them.
When Weohstan had breathed his last,
Unto his son, these weapons passed
And all the treasures, bright and grand
Were his, as well as plots of land.
He never had before that day
Adorned that armor, felt it weigh
His body down in safety's guard,
Nor touched its edges, taut and hard,
Nor had he drawn that ancient sword,
5220   Until called Beowulf, his lord,
Into the open battle-door,
Inviting him to fight the war.

But in the midst of what he felt,
The soldier's spirit did not melt,
Nor did his weapon drop in shame

When battling the dragon's flame,
And lo, the creature came to learn
The human's valor would not turn,
Nor would his blade withdraw its sting
5230    When fighting for his fallen king.
The dragon came to know this well
When greeting Wiglaf's battle yell.

And Wiglaf wore a weighted heart,
Disgraced by those who split apart
The warring group, no more reserved,
And said what each of them deserved:
"I think of days we sat to drink,
Escaping thoughts we dared not think.
For there within our Master's call,
5240    We drank and sung within his hall,
And bragged unto the means, we toasted,
Saying much, those times we boasted
Of the brave, untiring way
Our swords would serve, how we would say
To Beowulf our arms would be
United for his eyes to see,
Exposing might amid each deed,
Should Beowulf express the need,
That thane who dressed us in accord
5250    With weapons, armor, and each sword.
Not one of us refused the fact
Together we all made a pact
To give him back his love some day,
And for his kindness to repay
Him everything and every whim—
We swore our very lives to him.
He chose us from his boldest men,
Allowed us rank and brought us in,
Believing all our promises,
5260    Convinced our swords were just as his.
He made us soldiers, better men.
He meant to face the beastly grin
Himself, our lord and gracious liege,
To take upon himself the siege
Of dragon flame without the aid
Of any, thus his might displayed
Would rival that of days gone by
When all he did would catch the eye
And heart of men who came in length
5270    To marvel o'er our lordship's strength.

Although he keeps his noble charm,
The time has come for younger arms
To help the man who fights alone,
To be his muscle and his bone.
See now the flames that sear his skin,
So hear me out, and listen men,
The time has come, so let us bring
Our swords and aid this noble king!
By God Almighty, in my turn,
5280    I'd rather see myself to burn
Than watch my lord endure those flames.
Can any here fulfill his claims,
For who are we to leave the fight
And hold our guarding spheres uptight
Before his foe, ours as well,
Has not been ushered down to Hell,
And travel home as if complete,
While Beowulf stands in this heat?
The king does not deserve this fate,
5290    To stand alone before the gate
Of death amid the dragon's jaw,
A morsel for the beast to gnaw
And chew until his flesh is gone.
We swore our lives before his throne,
The armor, and each beaming sword,
We pledged to serve in his accord,
The same, our own within his call,
As one to benefit us all!"

5300    Then Wiglaf held aloft his sword
Espousing Beowulf, his lord,
With words of hope while diving through
The dragon's deadly flaming hue,
The fumes embodying his shape
As if an effervescent cape:
"My kingly lord, remember when
You boasted once before the men,
Aspiring in your gloried name
That you would never lose your fame.
5310    Believe me here, and fight for it,
Be strong, my lord, and never quit,
My glory king, protect and serve
Your life and fame as you deserve.
By every means, to save your pride,
My sword and I are at your side!"

The dragon drank those words in hate
When hearing Wiglaf's tongue relate
His oath to Beowulf, who lay
Before the dragon's fiery spray,
5320    The flaming hater of all men,
A fuming creature of chagrin;
It lunged amid its burning blow,
Ambitious to undo its foe.
Eruptive waves of fire swept
Around the shield that Wiglaf kept
Aloft amid the feral blast,
Until its wood, aflame at last,
Disintegrated into dust,
An ashy form he could not trust.
5330    His shining mail it served no more,
But sometime moving just before
The wooden oval shape combusted,
Wiglaf pushed by one he trusted,
Joining Beowulf behind
His iron shield's full metal bind.

And then that gloried warlord king
Arose, renewed, remembering
The days of old, when he was young,
For noble deeds, and banners hung,
5340    Compelling him again to lift
His master blade, that gracious gift,
An ancient relic come to be
His battle blade, his guarantee,
That *Naegling*, worn again, unleashed
From by his side where it lay, sheathed,
Unfettered, swung with skillful might,
Uniting in a stinging bite
Delivering in painful dread
A blow unto the dragon's head.
5350    But *Naegling* shattered, lost command,
As did each blade to join his hand.
In truth, the strength within his arms
Undid the iron, offered harm
To crafting of the forge's heat,
All due to Beowulf's defeat,
For nothing forged within the flame
Could match his strength, nor make it tame.
He often swung their shining gleam
In battle-hardened bloodshed's stream,
5360    But fate decreed their metal sting

Would fail to serve the Geat's king,
And thus amid this true conception,
There would be no need for weapons
In the glory of the one
Who sought to seek the beast undone.

The dragon lunged in anger's flare,
Erupting its volcanic fare.
Immersed in convoluting pain,
No longer would the beast abstain,
5370    Thus crazed and brutal in its fight,
It shed all fear amid its flight.
Its eager eyes beheld the chance,
And with the given circumstance,
It dove below, albeit a brief
Encounter, yet it sunk its teeth
Into the open fleshy space
To offer Beowulf disgrace,
Into his neck, the fangs prevailed;
He wobbled, for his sword had failed,
5380    And from the burning, boiling pain,
His blood spewed like the pouring rain.

## 38

And when the need for help grew nigh,
And Beowulf prepared to die,
The noble Wiglaf offered aid,
His guts and nerve, and strength displayed
In daring boldness ever worn
As from the day that he was born.
Ignoring acrid flames that spread
Each time the dragon shook its head,
5390    Assistance to his fallen lord
Came with the striking of his sword
Unto the unprotected spot
Below the neck, and though the hot
And scorching flames the dragon spewed
Engulfed his hand, his aim held true,
And in the sword plunged ever deep,
Which struck the chords within the keep
Internally, evicting fire,
Causing heat to fast expire,
5400    Thus dying out, no more to spew.
And from his side, the old king drew

His battle-blade, a jagged knife,
Convinced to take the dragon's life.

That bloody, battle laden king
Retained his wits among all things,
And knowing well what must be done,
Began to carve the fallen one.
In haste, he hacked the dragon's hide
In half, a fatal, fast divide.
5410    Defeated by their bravery,
The two akin to chivalry
Conjoined their efforts with each breath
To bring the dragon down to death.
Yet every action of those two
Expresses what each man should do
When times arise, and troubles brew,
Together, joined to see things through!

However, as the tide would turn,
No further glory would he earn,
5420    As Beowulf began to sever
Ties with living altogether.

Now the depths of dragon fangs
Began to swell, and searing pangs
Erupted from those toothy bites,
Convulsing in a raging spite
Around his neck; he felt them grow,
And inwardly, he seemed to know.
He sensed the stirring, ardent pain
As something surged throughout each vein,
5430    And Beowulf did not delight
In knowing venom from the bite
Was taking over in his blood,
Cascading like a summer flood.
He fumbled o'er his feet to find
A wall, embraced and unrefined
In every action's coming course,
As vision blurred in its divorce,
The while the pain would sear and jab,
Thus Beowulf, upon a slab
5440    Of stone, unwound and slowly dropped;
Above him where his body stopped
Were stony arches looming high,
As well as posts to catch the eye,

Which held aloft the rooftop's mold
Within that giant great hall's hold.

Then Wiglaf knelt to gently bathe
His bloody king, till proud and brave,
Though worn and beaten, nestled down,
And took the war-cap from his crown.

5450    Then Beowulf began to speak,
Despite the fact he had grown weak
From surging venom underneath
His flesh, and now his time was brief,
Accepting he had would be no more
A part of Midgard's wonder store,
For life was slipping in between,
And he had seen all to be seen
As was designed by God's own hand;
Not long, and he would leave his land,
5460    No pleasure left to fill his cup,
As soon he would be lifted up:
"I'd give this armor to a son,
But God has granted not a one,
No heir to claim my everything,
No child born thus to be a king,
Aspiring from an empty womb
As now I reach into my tomb.
For fifty winters, on my head
I wore my crown and knew no dread:
5470    No people from across the sea
Set forth a threatening decree
Upon the Geats' fertile soil,
Nor sent in soldiers for war's toils,
Hence speaking words of wicked deed.
My days have passed as fate decreed,
Awaiting time to pass me by
While ruling with a watchful eye
The best I could, no uttered swear,
Nor liar's war, obscene, unfair,
5480    Have I engaged my people in,
Avoiding wickedness and sin.
My breathing slows, but here I leave
In happiness, and do not grieve,
For God has never seen my sword
Bear inward on my people's horde,
Nor have I bathed in their own blood,
Nor kicked among them filth and mud.

Beloved one, Wiglaf, heed this measure,
Seeking fast the dragon's treasure:
5490   We destroyed its wretched hold,
And thus we own its gems and gold.
Be swift, away, and please deliver
Shining armor, olden silver,
Gold and gems, that I may spy
These wonders here before I die.
My death will come to me in ease,
To leave my kin, my land and seas,
If now my eyes can peer upon
This last great prize that we have won."

## 39

5500   The son of Weohstan complied,
And Beowulf was not denied,
For Wiglaf went in speedy suit
Of dispossession's ample loot,
Within the dark and gloomy hole
Of which his master took control,
Intent to raid and pluck the hoard,
Composed in mail and ready sword.
Embellished by his battle win,
He felt his way once deep within,
5510   A soldier of the noble sort,
A hero of his lordship's court,
And rapidly, ere he began,
He came upon the greater span
Of gems and gold upon the floor,
The scattered cups, and so much more,
Like armor rusting in the group,
Long gone from some old warring troupe,
And helmets shining in the den
Where lay the bones of many men,
5520   As well as other things gone dim
Without a hand to polish them.
Remaining where the dragon kept
Their presence when he duly slept,
No single piece save one escaped,
And thus the beaming gold pile draped
The way it had so long ago;
The dragon's death freed it for show.
(Thus gold can win, defeating those
Who trap themselves within its throws,

5530    Despite the depth it may reside,
        Or any way that it may hide!)

        When Wiglaf peered above his head,
        He spied a standard's golden thread,
        A craftsman's wonder by design,
        Allotted in the dragon's shrine.
        And from its weave, a golden light
        Erupted o'er all in his sight,
        A shining ray on every measure,
        Hall to wall, the floor and treasure.
5540    Not a creature stirred within,
        No other monsters bore their skin;
        The hoard was his to stock and store,
        He gathered gold, and gems, and more,
        From every pile's full glowing manner,
        Plates and cups, the glowing banner,
        Works of giants now deceased,
        Yet still their works surprised and pleased,
        And taking all his arms would hold,
        He filled them full of ancient gold.
5550    The dagger in those mighty hands,
        That weapon wielded in his stand,
        What Beowulf used to destroy
        The fire-breather's flaming ploy
        That once had guarded o'er the place,
        The tower and its golden grace
        Within the depths and deepest trend;
        The Geat king brought to an end
        The waging wings which wielded war,
        And killed that breath upon his shore,
5560    Forever halting flaming raids,
        No more upon the land displayed.

        Then Wiglaf ran in restless haste,
        In hopes his time was not a waste,
        And Beowulf still held to life,
        The same way he held to his knife
        When carving out the beastly hide,
        Empowered, firm, and full of pride,
        So that the treasure they acquired
        He would see as he desired.
5570    Hoping, praying, Wiglaf ran,
        A worried, worn and anxious man,
        Concerned that Beowulf, his king,
        Had died beneath the dragon's sting.

Arriving with the weighted stash
Amid his speedy, steady dash,
The fighter found his bleeding lord
In need of air, and dumped the hoard
Of all within his loaded arms
To comfort Beowulf from harm,
5580 And though his king was growing weak,
With muddled sounds, he tried to speak.
So Wiglaf bathed his dying king
In water from an ancient spring,
Unlocking in his vocal chords
The words within his wounded lord,
As heavy breathing in the breast
Of Beowulf's restricted chest
Unleashed the heavy hint of words
That soon in Wiglaf's ears were heard.

5590 Beholden for the treasure's heap,
He loosed the language from its keep:
"I thank the Lord of everything,
That great and giving Glory-king,
For He, the Maker of the earth
Has blessed my people in His mirth—
For all the golden, shining hoard
His mercy has seen to afford,
For all His grace has given me,
This beaming stock my eyes now see,
5600 Allowing me before my death
To speak upon my dying breath
The joy of sharing everything
Received by all from me, their king.
My life has bought this gleaming lot,
This hoard it seems that time forgot,
But gladly have I paid the price,
And did so without thinking twice.
I leave this now for Geatland,
This gold we earned with both our hands,
5610 And Wiglaf, I ask, guard my throne,
Please help them, for my time has gone.
And when the flames atop the pyre
Will carry me within their fire,
Searing me until my skin
Has turned to ash and faded thin,
Then have a tomb designed to hold
My ashes in a cup of gold
Created by my peoples' hands,

To keep me near my Geatland.
5620    So build it here astride this ledge,
Afore you reach the water's edge,
So passers on the ocean's top
Obligingly will stare and stop,
Remembering my many deeds,
And slowing from their current speeds
Proclaim it *Beowulf's Hillock*,
Thus any passing by this rock
On ship, devoured by the mist
And darkness will ignite the gist
5630    Of all I was, and know this land
For all completed by my hands."

When words fell with a bloody speck,
The king removed from round his neck
That golden necklace from its place,
And passing by his swollen face,
That shining garment came before
His vassal, Wiglaf, given more,
The golden helmet, and the plates
Of metal mail in light of fate,
5640    And also given by his king
Were golden, beaming, shining rings,
And when these things had passed along,
The war-kin held them as his throng,
And then upon his heart, words fell,
When told to always use them well:
"You are the last one of our kind,
The Waegmundings, no more you'll find.
Our race has faded from its shard,
And evanesced from off Midgard,
5650    Our bold and brave have gone to rest
In scattered tombs, a fatal nest,
Devoid of light, and as I dim,
My time is done; I follow them."

And then the silence crept aboard
The vying Wiglaf's dying lord,
And nothing more escaped his lips,
As he embraced his final trip;
And soon his men would stack the wood,
And his shape would be gone for good
5660    Adrift amid the burning flame,
All crying o'er that greatest name.
His spirit flew from in his skin,

A soul released to join its kin,
And now the world would know the story,
All of Beowulf's great glory.

## 40

Wiglaf stood, a young one left
Without a king, alone, bereft,
And gazed upon the bloody drape
Of Beowulf's unmoving shape,
5670 A guard unto the fallen king.
But, too, the dragon felt the sting
Of death, and sliced in two remained
A cold and silent beast restrained.
The two had joined in one accord,
And with the coming of their swords
Had torn it in a fatal sweep
From down below in Midgard's keep,
As now it lay before the base
Of where its form had left the trace
5680 Of treasure, precious to the eye,
Before the place it came to die,
And when it fell unto the earth,
These men removed from in their girth
The means to slice the beast apart,
And cut it from its gut to heart.
The beast had ceased to tour the sky
At night, a symbol passing by
In terror, never more to burn
And glow within its hated urn,
5690 Devouring the riches kept
Beneath its form, now duly swept
Unto the ones who took its life
By way of honor and a knife.

No other men would brave the dare
Of flashing flame and venom where
The outcome would be bland and bleak,
No, theirs would not be one to speak,
For who could tame the booming bang
Of dragon lust and toothy fang,
5700 Or even take from in its hold
In stealth, the smallest piece of gold
The while the dragon lurked, awake;
No, who would put their lives at stake!

But Beowulf embraced the flame
And thus the gold was his to claim,
Acquired with his very blood
Amidst the battle's killing flood;
The dragon and the king arrived
At death, for neither had survived.

5710    And when the war came to a halt,
From in the wilderness's vault,
The men who claimed to be aboard
For Beowulf, their giving lord,
The cowards who betrayed their vow,
Exposed themselves in light of how
Their feeble bodies quaked for breath,
Arriving when the dragon's death
Became confirmed, abating fears,
And so they came, with droopy spears.
5720    A kindred lot of frightened fools,
Escaped the while the dragon's tools
Enflamed the land and slew their lord,
Despondency within their swords,
For not a one came to his aid,
And left his dying shape displayed,
Thus holding spears and javelins
Avoiding flight and kept within
Their grasp the while their master died,
Appearing, since they chose to hide,
5730    And showed their shameful faces then,
A group of ten ignoble men,
Compelled to move along the thread
To where their lord lay cold and dead,
All sorrowed and completely weak,
Awaiting for Wiglaf to speak.
He knelt before the lifeless hull
Of Beowulf, bereft and dull,
Espousing hope his lord would wake
By pouring water for the sake
5740    Of rousing Beowulf from sleep,
But could not, for his spirit's keep
Had gone where only God can grant.
He failed by trying to supplant
The death with life in every drop.
At length, the soldier came to stop.
He realized that none alive
Could bring him back to pulse and thrive,
Or move the matter God decreed.

The earth and men could not succeed
5750 In matters He Who ruled them all
Had given forth His final call,
For none abroad could speak nor spill
The means to change the Father's will,
For all are moved as He will see,
And this way it shall always be.

Then Wiglaf spun with anger's garb
And hung those men upon the barb,
Expressing to them for their fear
The words a coward needs to hear.
5760 The war-kin's soul fell burdened down,
And thus he spoke betwixt a frown
The very words concerned and true
That came as what he had to do:
"I speak what any man would say
In truth to you this very day.
The one you swore your very lives
If needed, he whose body strives
For burning on the open pyre
Within the raging honor fire,
5770 This man gave you everything
You tarnish, swords, and mail and rings;
You sat upon his mighty bench,
A boastful lot, but now your stench
Is filth and illness in my gut,
An endless spasm in a rut,
For there, he opened up his hands
And filled your wealth by his commands,
And helmets, brass, and shiny gold
Were given, yours, each one to hold,
5780 But you who took the best of weapons
Sundered forth in vile deception.
War arose, and did you stand?
Not you, I say, no, not this band!
In panic, yellow streaks applied,
For lo, our leader was denied
As like a dog with tails tucked in,
You took your swords, embraced chagrin
As if it were a merry thing,
Abandoning your very king!
5790 Were he alive, would he now boast
Of all his men who once gave toast?
Not hardly, but with God's own grace,
He stood alone in danger's face

And swung his blade to seek revenge
While you hid in your yellow cringe!
What aid I gave to lend our lord
Was nothing, but I gave my sword.
I came to him, in thoughtful keep,
And knew none but our king could sweep
5800    The evil thing away from here,
my sword found luck within the sphere
Beneath the dragon's flaming chords
Within its neck, thus went my sword
And made the blazing burning flame
To halt forever ere it came.
The lot of you refused to come,
And soon forgot where you came from,
And thus our king embraced his death
Alone beneath the dragon's breath.
5810    And now, no blades or rings or land
Will come from out our giver's hands,
All over now for me and you,
And anyone you ever knew
Who shares with you a bloodline's bond:
When other Geats, brave and fond
Of battle, hear how you all fled
And left our king the while he bled,
Your race will have its end of you,
And nothing but your lives will do,
5820    For death itself would better be
Than living life for those to see
Who hear of how you turned your face,
And walk abroad in your disgrace!"

# 41

Then Wiglaf bade a herald go
Across the crag and never slow
Until he reached the other side
Where Geats waited, sick inside,
A morning's ride away from him,
Awaiting news to come to them,
5830    Unknowing if their king survived,
If Beowulf still pulsed and thrived,
Or met an end beneath the flame
Of one his sword could never tame,
But still those men let hope survive
And prayed their king was still alive.

The herald bade his horse move on,
And came to make his message known,
Explaining to those men at last
The present and the recent past:
5840    "Our king has gone from all his people,
Slain beneath the dragon's evil,
Though the creature died as well,
Divided by the dagger's knell;
The enemy will fly no more
And sleeps within its bloody gore.
No blade could dent its scaly hide,
Nor penetrate it deep inside.
There Wiglaf waits in mourning still,
The son of Weohstan grown ill
5850    By Beowulf's unmoving side,
A tired soldier, sad, denied,
And watching o'er our fallen king
A soldier weary, sad to bring
Such news abroad, these words I've said,
As he sits where those two lay, dead.
And now this race of people can
Expect to greet each warring man,
Those Franks and Frisians learning how
Our lord has passed before us now.
5860    The news will burn like dragon's fire,
O'er the seas, after the pyre
Has turned the body of our king
Into the ashes we will bring
Into the tomb we must prepare.
Yea, words of this will travel there.
Our former king, bold Hygelac,
Exposed us to this warring track
By feuding with the Hugas, and
The Hetware, all by his command,
5870    For he decided and displayed
His power in his distant raids
When riding up the river Rhine
With soldiers and a danger sign
Until a larger force amassed
And slew him when his vessel passed,
Thus Hygelac succumbed to slumber,
Beaten by the foes' shear numbers,
Taken down, a final fall,
And brought no treasure to his hall.
5880    So from our raids upon those banks,

We knew no friendship with the Franks.
Nor can we think to share our mead
With anyone we call a Swede.
We all know Ongentheow's past,
How Haethcyn hit him with a blast
And wounded him near Ravenswood,
When over eager Geats stood
For war against the vying Swedes.
Then Ongentheow fought with speed,
5890    Though old, returning blow for blow,
And wrought the end in anger's throw,
Disposing of the Geat's kin,
Thus laying low our brave Haethcyn,
And rescued then his captured wife,
As well as took our brave king's life.
He looted all in his attack,
And sent our soldiers running back
Into the hold of Ravenswood,
Intent to give them nothing good.
5900    Their bodies, weak and weary worn
Were thrown into the wood and thorn.
But Ongentheow and his men
Encircled round the wooded glen
And boasted long into the night
To those who had so taken flight
Into the woods, a fearful band
Entrapped behind the foe's command.
Then Ongentheow spoke his mind,
And swore some men his hand would bind
5910    Within the morning's coming tide,
A gift for all the birds outside,
For he would gut them as they hung,
And then he further pressed his tongue
By saying at his very best
He then would handle all the rest.
But with the sun came shining rays
As trumpets blared a song of praise
By way of Hygelac's resort,
A battle yell of soldier sport,
5920    And men again felt gladness ring
As came support from their brave king
Along with men supporting them,
And broke the dawn on spirits dim."

**42**

"Then bloody strands fell all around
As both the bands of Geats found
The Swedes and joined in battle rounds,
On every side upon those grounds,
And swords and shields sung battle hymns
As many died because of them.
5930    And Ongentheow had to give
The order that his men might live,
And forced aback to higher ground,
They stood behind his fortress, sound
In make and mark, for he had heard
The many daunting, leering words
Expressing that his foe, in length,
Came full and well with mighty strength.
Of Hygelac, the old king knew
Within the openness, askew
5940    Would be his arm, and he would fail,
But knowing this helped him prevail
Within his mind, for those behind
His caring guard his might would bind,
Those Swedish wives and children, too,
He would protect, and so they knew
His sword was theirs, and so would swing
When meeting with the Geat king.
His bravery was not benign,
But wisdom gave his heart a sign,
5950    And thus he fled and gave the call
To flee behind his earthen wall.
The Geats pushed and swept the field,
Convinced behind each sword and shield,
Then smashed the walls that kept them out,
Exuding forth a warring shout
Within their eager battle manner,
Waving Hygelac's proud banner.
Then the gray-haired lord's dismay
Came full when he was brought to bay,
5960    The Geat swords upon his throat,
A measure to extort and gloat,
And Eofor brought judging wrath
Upon the Swedish lord's new path.
The first to bring his weapon's might
Upon the Swede and join the fight
Was Wulf, who hit him angrily,
And cracked his war-cap openly;
And thus the old king found his blood

Burst open like a dawning flood
5970 That poured the length of his gray hair.
But Ongentheow showed them there
No fear within: he swiftly turned
And in his wrath, at once returned
A blow unto the one who struck,
And did so wildly, bracing luck,
For his, in deed was twice as strong
As was the one which sung its song
Unto his helmet, breaking grate.
But soon would turn the hands of fate,
5980 And Wulf received the same he gave,
A wounded skull, no more to crave
The battle, as he tried to raise
His blade, but fell within a daze,
As blood erupted from the spot
Where steel had entered, burning hot.
Though deeply cut inside his head,
This time, brave Wulf escaped the dead
As fate allowed, and he lived on.
To Eofor, this was not known,
5990 And thus he rushed on faith, reliant,
Holding his blade carved by giants,
Smashing through the shield's relief
A passing moment, ever brief,
And as the shards of wood and steel
Collided, dropping to a kneel,
The Swedish king behind that guard
Was hit beneath the weapon hard,
Embedded in his chest on through,
Then swiftly came the sword anew
6000 In battle's gleam, a bloody red,
And Ongentheow fell down dead.
The tide had turned, and on the field
The Geats, spurned, began to wield
Their swords the likes of none before,
And quickly brought themselves before
Their fallen Wulf to lend a hand,
And bandaged him, then helped him stand.
His brother took with ample speed
The coating of that olden Swede,
6010 His mail, his sword, his ancient gear,
He quickly made it disappear
From off the body of the man
Whose life had reached its final span,
So, from the war-cap to the sword,

He brought them all to his new lord.
Then Hygelac bade welcome be
These men before him openly,
And warmly blessed their every deed,
Embracing them with caring need,
6020    A thanks gone out upon his lips,
Well worded for their warring trip,
Expressed before his peoples' ears,
Configured so that all would hear,
And giving such an oath to say
Within his mead-hall on that day
When all returned, the treasure hoard
Would open up to thank each sword.
His words, in length, spun on that day
Said soon their deeds he would repay
6030    And raise them high for better health
By offering abundant wealth,
And give them gold and silver rings,
Rewarding them, as was the king's
Own way to have his thanks displayed
For what they did by way of blade.
And more, for Eofor's delight,
The king gave word that very night
His daughter was to be his wife,
And thus he pledged to him her life.
6040    The battles stirring o'er this feud
Are boiling in that Swedish brood,
No doubt intent when they have learned
The fires took our lord and burned
His body, gone as they profess
The Geats wander leaderless,
Without their king, the greatest one,
That Beowulf—his hand undone,
The one who kept the foes abroad
From setting foot upon our sod,
6050    Who was the best of all the thanes,
Who aided Hrothgar and his Danes—
The very one whose life we sing
And praise, the bravest Geat king.
Then let us ride before that lord
To seek his form in flame's accord
To swiftly burn the flesh from him.
The fire melts as well those gems
And gold: take all that horrid heap
And place it in that fire's keep,
6060    Those cups and rings, the treasure flood

He purchased with his very blood.
Involve the flames upon that stash,
Until they are but scattered ash.
No one alive should have the joy
Of having in their own employ
Those items won by death's accord,
Not any gold, nor ancient sword.
No woman should accept a gem,
No necklace worn by one of them,
6070    No golden anthem shining loud
By any one should be allowed,
Instead they all should not be glad,
And hang their heads in manners sad
Within a hundred lands' accord,
For losing Beowulf our lord,
No laughter from their mourning lips,
Forever gone the way time slips
From all when death commands its might,
And sends one to that endless night.
6080    For laughter will forever be
A silent notion loosed from he
Who gave his life that all would thrive,
That final promise when alive
The master o'er the Geats gave,
But of himself, he could not save,
And nothing more this life can hold,
Not treasures held of gem and gold
Will give him light, for all is dim,
Thus joy has gone from out of him.
6090    A many morn shall spears awake
Within the hands or those who take
The words I speak and swallow them,
Forsaken lot, the hollow whim,
As every hand that has a spear
Will throw them, and no one will hear
The harp's soft song, no warming awe,
Instead, the raven's languid caw
Expressed to welcome in its thread
The present coming of the dead,
6100    Intent to sing among its regal
Deathly suit unto the eagle
How it packed its cackle-bill
With corpses to its very fill,
And crammed its feather ridden gut
With bodies tossed among its rut

With speed the wolves could never match,
Exuberant o'er every catch."

And so the herald spoke his mind;
The echo stung in words not kind,
6110    For he was brave in what he said,
And ugly errand overhead,
But one of truth, and nothing less
In all the man came to profess.

Then soldiers rose, and walked below
The cliff in manners soft and slow,
Envisioning the glory sights,
And wept before the fallen might
Of Beowulf, there on the sand,
Beneath the net of death's command,
6120    That giver of all golden rings,
Deceased and gone, their loving king.
His days were gone, this Geat lord,
But even with a broken sword,
He drew aback the dragon's breath,
And ended in a noble death.
But first, they spied the dragon's form,
Lain out before the tower dorm
That once had been its domicile,
That scaly, multi-colored, vile
6130    Behemoth stretched for fifty feet,
Burnt blue beneath its very heat,
And from the sun, its color shone,
Though cut in half unto its bone.
The fifty feet that claimed its length
Had stilled beneath the war-king's strength,
Though once it flew amid the heights,
A terror born in darkened fright,
Imposing hate upon all men,
Then diving to its primal den.
6140    Now death belayed it from its flight.
It had no home to guard with might,
Nor treasure like the shining cup
Which caused its dreadful waking up,
No plates or mail for it to catch,
Forever hidden by its latch,
A rusted lot of metal bliss,
The likes the world would never miss.
For buried down within the center,
There it sat, a thousand winters,

6150 Or the wanderer might think.
  And all of this, no man could drink,
  For every stone and every gem
  Had magic binding all of them.
  Nay, none alive could claim the power
  To encroach that hidden tower,
  Entering the hidden door
  Where golden loot and much, much more
  Could only be expounded on
  Should God above atop His throne
6160 Unwind the truth, and part the path,
  Preventing them from deathly wrath
  By way of it, the dragon-beast,
  And have its mysteries released.
  Yea, none save He Who watches men
  Could open up the monster's den,
  Almighty God moved earth and stone
  To let the man atop the throne
  Of Geatland command its center,
  Giving him the strength to enter,
6170 Making all of this yet known
  To him, and only him alone.

## 43

  The hidden treasure that they saw
  Was buried deep, and broke God's law,
  The way the dragon knew it would
  In fact had done the beast no good.
  Though it had beaten Wiglaf's lord,
  Still death came from its lorded hoard
  For hiding in its darkened hole,
  The beast was done, without its soul.
6180 What man can say when life is done,
  The strongest or the bravest one,
  To leave behind an empty hall,
  Disposed of when death comes to call?
  So Beowulf engaged a fight
  And suffered from the dragon's bite,
  Unknowing of what God decreed,
  Or that his death would come with speed,
  Or that the reasons passing by
  Would never truly answer why.
6190 And so the magic tread its course

By men long dead in their divorce
From earthly ties; from living's way;
No more upon the earth to stay;
The punishment was meant to be
For judgment day, that last decree
From God Himself, the one He said,
The one left for that day of dread.
Whoever took from off that lot
Would end up in the burning hot
6200 Commencement of the deepest well
Amid the flames and blaze of Hell,
Engorged with sin and guilt, indeed,
If what allured him there was greed.
No one but God could break the chain
Of magic guarding that domain,
And synchronize His wonder plan,
Which opens up His grace to man.
And Beowulf did not abide
With lusting o'er the gems inside,
6210 And so his worth was proven o'er
The minute he stepped through its door.

Then Wiglaf spoke, Weohstan's son,
Before the men o'er what was done:
"How often does a man endure
The fate of all, one born so pure!
That time has come before us all:
We tried advising in our call
To him who governed everything,
That truest man, that faithful king,
6220 That guard and shield, protector o'er
This land we love from shore to shore,
Against the dragon and its flame,
Beneath the earth, intent to tame
The very beast that for so long
Had guarded o'er its wealthy throng,
And let it stay asleep and curled
Until the ending of the world.
But as you know the pull of fate
Was far too strong, nor would he wait,
6230 As in his will, he chose to fight,
Thus died beneath the dragon's bite.
We all can see the lorded hoard
That took the life of our great lord,
But Beowulf was more in worth
Than all the riches on the earth.

And so the gift he left us all
Was one unworthy of his fall.
That gold, and more, my eyes have seen,
That tower's hull, fit for the glean,
6240    Where gems and swords and armor, too,
Were hidden from our peoples' view,
Espied the time the war was done.
I came to seek them, everyone,
And gathered up their shining charm,
Each piece it took to fill my arms,
That gold and silver, everything
To bring before our dying king.
He lay alive, his head down hung,
But still his mind and speaking tongue
6250    Were held in tact. He spoke to me
And asked within his sad decree
To greet you all, and to ensure
In order that his name endure,
To tell you all to take his ash
And keep it as a sacred stash
Within a tower to consume
His memory, a wonder tomb—
As great in make up as his fame,
To herald forth his glory name,
6260    When Beowulf himself still walked
O'er Midgard, and his splendor talked
Of all his deeds, the lot of them,
Which said no man could dare match him.
Now all, come forth and enter in
The tower, see the dragon's sin,
The measure of its shining chime,
And look upon it one last time.
I will go first and lead the way,
That each of you can duly say
6270    Your eyes beheld the golden shape
Of gems and silver in their drape,
And every piece, those gleaming rings,
As well as many other things.
Now light the flame and spark the fire,
So prepping thus our keeper's pyre:
As soon as all have seen the hoard,
Our hands will carry forth our lord,
And set him in the heats refine,
Forever kept in God's design."

6280   Then Wiglaf chose those Geat men
        Whose wealth was great, and asked again
        To those amassing land and gold
        To follow him as they were told
        In order to do one last good,
        And asked them to bring to him wood
        Which they would light with brightest fire;
        Offer Beowulf a pyre:
        "Amid the heat, the flame will dine
        Upon this passing king of mine,
6290   The fire, black, round his profile,
        The one who saw the arrows pile
        In torrid fits the likes of rain
        Which poured in raids without refrain,
        Those iron tips in barbed effect,
        Which fell in feathered ends, direct
        And sharp upon the blocking shield
        Within the flood that would not yield,
        The arrows shot erupting through
        Those linden shapes without renew,
6300   The storming wrath devoid of stopping
        Felt in arrows ever dropping."

        Taking seven of his best,
        All chosen at Wiglaf's behest,
        He led them down into the hole
        Where treasure hid below the knoll
        Awaited without any fear,
        Without a dragon to appear;
        The one who led held in his hand
        A glowing torch to lead the band.
6310   Those chosen, Beowulf's delight,
        Went swiftly underneath that light:
        And there beneath its heated glow,
        The Geats' eyes came to bestow
        Their furtive glance upon the heaps
        Of gold and gems within that keep.
        But not a beast or dragon's hide
        Was left to guard the shining pride
        Embedded deep within the place
        Where one had ruled without God's grace.
6320   But fearless now, the Geats turned,
        And while the torchlight amply burned,
        They gathered treasure in each hand
        And moved it up upon their land.
        The dragon's lifeless corpse was rolled

Unto the cliff to be extolled
By crashing waves, gone out to sea
Adrift and taken openly,
No more a sight before the eyes
As in the ocean's compromise,
6330    The beast would sink and rot and float,
As passers by would gladly gloat
That Beowulf, that best of men
Had triumphed and had done it in.
Then with the passing of the dragon,
Treasure placed within a wagon
Next to Beowulf was brought,
And taken to the sand, they sought
To place his form upon the fire
Giving them the burning pyre.

## 44

6340    A heap of wood was ready made,
And all around the shields displayed
Aside the helmets and the mail
Erected to their posts by nail
Expressed his word and would consign
Their Beowulf, his last design.
The bearers took their lord and king,
And working through their teary sting,
Applied his body as they could
Upon the stack of readied wood.
6350    And then the soldiers lit the flame,
That greatest pyre which held the frame
Of Beowulf, set on the stack,
Then smoke arose both thick and black,
And when the wind unleashed its gust,
The flame blazed higher in its lust
To drink the blood and sear the flesh
Of one caught in its blazing mesh,
The while the heat beat down and kept
Their leader's form as many wept
6360    Until at last the flame rushed on
And Beowulf was finally gone.
The Geats stayed, no time to borrow,
Laden with their inward sorrow,
Caring not for anything,
Except the loss of their great king.
Before the flaming, burning light,

A woman with her hair wound tight,
Expressed in grayness, full of age,
Responded by the flaming stage
6370    By singing such a mournful tune
As any heard for many moons,
Bewailing o'er the coming days
Of frightful lust and foreign plays
Where none of Geatland could win,
Entrapped betwixt the warring sin
Of others lording power's reign,
Encroaching on their vast domain
To terrorize and capture them,
A fading remnant going dim.
6380    Then Heaven drank the bulging smoke
The while the woman mourned and spoke.

The Geats piled the stones up high,
Entreating Beowulf's reply
To Wiglaf, making strong and tall
The tower seen before them all
So men upon the water-road
Could see its sight and let it goad
Each vessel on from far and wide,
A monument of earthly pride;
6390    For ten days, men worked tirelessly
To build the tower all would see,
And placed his ashes in the cup
Of gold before they sealed it up
Within the walls made firm and high
With willing hands glad to comply.
When this was done, the items won
By him and Weohstan's brave son
By beating back the dragon's flame
And garnishing a mighty fame
6400    Were placed within, those gold and rings
Those necklaces, and shining things,
The armor and each hammered sword—
All taken from the dragon's hoard,
Were left there, too the silver, jewels,
All they knew, those wealth-like tools
From in that stash before the band
Of men was buried in the sand,
Into the earth to once again
Be of no use to any man.

6410    The bravest twelve of every man
Rode horses round the tower's span,
Those Geats with a noble mark
To tell their tales amid the sparks
Remaining in their beating hearts,
Reciting songs in lengthy parts
Of Beowulf, their greatest king,
Of his greet honor, yet to sing
Again for all his might deeds.
They spun about on their great steeds,
6420    And praised him for his honored fame,
And spoke of greatness in his name.
So every man should say the things
They feel in honor for their kings,
With love and kindness to bestow
Upon their leader, ere he goes
And leaves behind his corpse's shape,
The while his soul at last escapes
To join with others by and by
Unto that sacred place on high.

6430    And so it was that many men
Rode round and round, again, again,
Those left behind to wail and mourn
Their king, left broken and forlorn
O'er Beowulf, their most loved lord,
And said aloud in one accord
No greater king had walked the land,
No prince whose giving, loving hand
Had held aloft its peoples' needs,
And done so without lust or greed,
6440    Deserving every bit of praise,
Unending, sung for many days.

## Epilogue: The Wanderer

"The lonely one devoid of space
At times revives within the grace
Of God, although his heavy heart
Involved in naught must make a start,
And for a time, its length unknown
Move by his hand upon the throne
Of earthly waterway's decree,
Upon the icy, chilly sea,
6450    Uncertain of its endless mile,

The path of one in his exile.
By way of sea and loss of trust,
Events will go what way they must!"
So said the wanderer o'er each

And every heartache felt to breech
His yearning locked somewhere within,
Despondent o'er the death of kin:

"Quite often, I would speak alone
Of trouble to myself, unknown
6460    To any other, ere the light
Erupted, breaking through the night.
And now, no one alive is worth
My thoughts, no, none upon this earth.
I know the deepest truth of men,
That noble ones keep down within
The fabric of their every thought
Within their minds a reason sought
By none, save them, a guarded hoard
Of mental fabric they adored,
6470    And thus think as he wishes to.
And by the time that fate is through,
The weary spirit cannot stand,
Nor can the saddened mind command
The grasp of what its sees and feels.
Those seeking fame appear surreal,
But weighed within their chamber-chest
Are dreary thoughts within their breast;
So I, alone and sorrow filled,
Without my home, my kinsmen killed,
6480    Have bound in chains my deepest mind,
Somewhere that only I can find,
Since many winters long ago,
I placed my lord beneath the throw
Of earth and stone, that darkened sleep
Beneath the mound's forever keep,
And I, in desolation's grip
Retreated on an icy trip
Across the whale-road's frozen top,
En endless journey meant to stop
6490    When I, without a mead hall's bench,
Could taste the ale and firmly clench
My hands around some gift from him,
A giver of things never dim,
Of treasured rings and golden mugs,

A prince whose reach would pull and tug
Upon my heart, who knew my kin,
Or wished to let the friendless in,
To spare me from the lonely night,
And fill me with renewed delight.
6500 The ones like me can comprehend,
Those without love or any friend:
The path of exile keeps him down,
No gold upon his weary crown,
A spirit cold, withdrawn from mirth,
Refuting wealth that comes from earth.
He thinks of war-kin in the hall,
And treasure given to them all,
When he was young, that golden hoard
Adorning him, as from his lord
6510 The golden heap was opened up,
And more, he filled his every cup
With mead and as the joy released,
He learned the manner he should feast.
But now, bereft at all espied,
He cried aloud that joy has died!

And so he knows the bitter truth,
That he must go without reproof,
Forego his days without a lord
To lift a shield and wave a sword:
6520 Then sorrow mingles in with sleep,
And holds this loner in its keep,
Confining thus this lonesome one
In every measure he has done.
His weary mind embraces thoughts
Of serving one no longer sought,
That perished king and greatest lord,
And still he sinks in this accord,
Imagining the things he said
As gently he lays down his head
6530 Upon master's bended knee,
Just as before, done openly,
When he was young, and joy was known,
And he could sit beside the throne.
And then the man without a friend
Awakes and sinks and tries to mend,
The while he watches sea birds bathe
Exuberantly with each lathe
For beak while pruning feather's stock,
While snow and hail fall down like rocks.

6540    Then falls the grief that holds its weight
        Much heavier within the fate
        That beats along the heart's defeat,
        When longing for his lord's retreat,
        That sacred place he served in joy,
        No longer in his lord's employ.
        So sorrow comes again in force,
        A memory without divorce
        When bringing back the dead again,
        Those long remembered next of kin.
6550    He sees and greets them, every one,
        Then waits and sees their forms undone
        As back away they fade and swim;
        Until no more in front of him.
        Those ghostly shapes cannot amount
        To much in means of deep account
        When conversation needs its place
        Within the confines of his space.
        And so, with care and fresh renew,
        The one is filled with what to do
6560    As weary worn he skips the grave
        While gliding o'er each icy wave.

        Indeed, I cannot comprehend
        Why darkness does not apprehend
        The spirit here within my chest,
        When many men, indeed the best,
        Before this world have gone in vain,
        And left their halls, each mighty thane.
        And so each day, this Midgard's sway
        Falls further into mass decay—
6570    So man cannot say he is smart
        Before his years have played their part,
        Imparting wisdom with his age,
        Upon the world's abundant stage.
        A wise man must incorporate
        The use of patience in his state
        Of being, and before he speaks
        Use wisdom, never being weak
        Or reckless when he takes his aim,
        Nor be too cheerful, let his name
6580    Be paired with greed, or full of boasts,
        That clearly he can see the coasts
        He sets before when dealing in
        The living will of unknown men.

A man must wait to speak his vow
Until the time he can see how
The proper end his proud heart beats
Will offer truth when made complete.
A hero wise and full of thought
Will see the price that gold is bought
6590    Within the terror it may bring,
When all the wealth has felt the sting
Of war and lies somewhere in waste,
A symptom of some hero's haste,
As Midgard stands the same in wreck,
Its walls and halls, each wooden deck
Engorged on winter's dying gift,
The snow and ice upon each lift,
The banners taken, worn and lost,
Corrupted by the teething frost,
6600    As wind swoops down, a sullen blast,
Decaying halls beneath their cast,
As many Thanes have gone to rest,
Deprived of joy, a fruitless jest,
And all, in fact, the very troop
Itself has gone within the scoop
Of war and wind beside the hall,
Beneath the shadow of the wall,
And when the bird took o'er the sea,
Another felt the deep melee
6610    Of what befell him in the fray
Of meeting with the wolf born gray
Which shared his life blood's dying breath
With bleakest dark, the coming death,
And one, the living could not save,
And he is buried in his grave.
And so, He came in anger's wrath
Destroying all along the path
Before the city, and within,
The One Who had created men,
6620    Until the echoes and the sounds
Of people fell in silent rounds
And emptiness exempted all,
That ancient, beaten giant's hall."

He stood aback and pondered long
On those foundations, wise and strong,
And on the darkness life can bring,
Exacting thoughts of distant things,
Remembering the conflicts gone,

And of the changing up of thrones,
6630    Expounding on the brave and week,
Then prompted, came again to speak:

"Where is the horse, and he who rides?
Where is the one whose wealth confides
In each of us, that giving lord?
Where are the benches we adored?
Where are the dreams and duty call
That claimed us there within that hall?
Alas for what has covered up
The shining glow of golden cups!
6640    Alas for what did not prevail,
Those soldiers gone within their mail!
Alas for all this pertinence
Which hails the loss of our loved prince!
Oh, how that time has come and gone
Beneath the cover of night's throne
As if the wonder of such men
Had never truly ever been!
What eyes will see in place of those,
The troops who once held firm their pose,
6650    Removed, replaced by change's call,
Now standing thus a wicked wall,
Extremely high in every bound
With colored serpents wound around.
By way of spears, the fighters fell,
Those gloried weapons left to tell
Amid their hunger and the greed
To slaughter all, as was their need,
That famous fate, the storm cloud's beat
Upon the rocky cliff's retreat,
6660    As falling frost retrains the earth,
The harbinger of winter's birth;
And then the darkness starts to seep,
While all around the shadows, deep,
Bring from the north a cruel chilling
As a hailstorm set for killing,
Wreaking malice and chagrin
Upon the many hosts of men.
The life of mankind has much danger,
Treating many as a stranger
6670    In this kingdom set on Midgard,
And the changes seem to hit hard
Underneath the heaven's awning.
Here the current issue dawning

Comes in way without retreating,
Seeing how one's wealth is fleeting,
Seeing how the friend is fleeting,
Seeing how man's life is fleeting,
Seeing how one's kin is fleeting,
And amid this notion's beating,
6680    That a life will end in haste,
The earth's foundations turned to waste!"

So spoke the man of wisdom's kind
Within the counsel of his mind.
How great is he who holds to trust,
A fighter knowing that he must
Entrap the longing and the grieving
In his breast, not yet relieving
What remains, until he knows
His path, quite certain where it goes—
6690    A hero must in every measure
Hold to courage as his treasure.
It is better for the one
Who seeks out mercy and not fun,
Who seeks the Father's consolation
From the heaven's vast duration,
Where for all who pass the test,
The final permanence will rest.

Printed in Great Britain
by Amazon